Dearest Marguerite

Dearest Marguerite

Letters from a Soldier
To the Wife
He Left Behind

Marguerite Swenson Young

iUniverse, Inc.
New York Lincoln Shanghai

Dearest Marguerite
Letters from a Soldier To the Wife He Left Behind

iUniverse books may be ordered through booksellers or by contacting:

iUniverse
2021 Pine Lake Road, Suite 100
Lincoln, NE 68512
www.iuniverse.com
1-800-Authors (1-800-288-4677)

ISBN: 978-0-595-47070-9 (pbk)
ISBN: 978-0-595-91352-7 (ebk)

Printed in the United States of America

Dedication:

To our four children:
Lois Abbuhl
Crystal Mach
Thomas Young
Nancy Moser

Special Recognition:

To my parents: George and Ruth Swenson, who invited me, their pregnant daughter to return to their Dawson, Minnesota farm home to live with them "for the duration" ... and to welcome their first granddaughter; and to Lyle's parents, Lester and Almeda Young, who regularly invited us to visit them in Granite Falls, Minnesota. Such family support was a great blessing to Lyle and to me. It represented families across the country in the total commitment to winning the war.

Acknowledgements

Lyle Young wrote letters to me, his wife, Marguerite (Margie), almost every day for nearly three years, from the time he was drafted, until the time he returned from Army Air Corps service in the South Pacific in November 1945. Excerpts from those letters and the pictures he sent made this book possible. Lyle says, "This is our story." In the process of my writing the original manuscript, he read books about the campaigns in the South Pacific, and noted references to experiences he knew well. He is pleased that "Dearest Marguerite" will be available to a wider readership.

Nancy Moser, our youngest daughter, is a successful writer of about twenty books. She retrieved my original manuscript from an aging floppy disk in 2006, and edited the copy when the possibility of publication was only a dream. She has continued to lend her advice in making her father's and my story a reality. I could not have done it without her encouragement and professional know-how. A million thanks, Nancy.

Our three daughters: Lois, Crys, and Nancy, in their annual retreat with their mom, designed the front and back covers of the book. Their enthusiasm and expertise made for a delightful evening. I thank them. They and our talented son Tom, make us proud parents.

Foreword

I am a saver of letters. Until I began writing Lyle's story, I could not know how important those letters would be. In 1995, Lyle and I reread his letters, written to me from his thirty-month service in the Army Air Corps in World War II.

Surprisingly, at the bottom of the pile was one envelope unopened. I held it to the light. Yes, there was a letter inside … it was the last letter he had sent from Okinawa, and he had returned home before the letter arrived! On a January day in 1995, fifty years after it had been sent, we opened it.

That winter, I wrote the story of Lyle's war years and made copies for our family, never intending the book to be published. Years passed, until my daughter, Nancy Moser reread her copy and called me, "Mother, this book should be published. It is a love story and it is history!" Two friends read excerpts and encouraged me. Annette Wiechert, a retired commander in the U.S. Navy, related that the Veteran's History Project in the Library of Congress in Washington, D.C., wants personal accounts of those momentous years. Jeanne Kern, a writing class friend and an author, called to say, "Go for it."

So readers, here it is … Marguerite

A bit of philosophy.

In retrospect, "Every day has been a gift. Every day still is."

Introduction

During this war, which is now called World War II, Lyle Young left his family in Minnesota and was sent around the world to fight Japan. His only contact with his wife and family was through letters. There were no long distance telephone calls and no furloughs back home. Once in the service you were in "for the duration".

It was a long war. And he was only twenty-two years old …

As a soldier in the Army Air Corps it was the duty of his Service Squadron to repair and service the airplanes that bombed Japanese installations over the vast Pacific.

The following is a very personal—yet in many ways a very universal—history of one soldier, Lyle Young, as he experienced a unique part of his life while holding onto his dreams for the future while I, the love of his life, his Marguerite, waited for him at home …

* * * *

Lyle and I met at the University of Minnesota in the winter of 1941. He graduated that June and took a job with the Pennsylvania Railroad in Pittsburgh, Pennsylvania. Our friendship had blossomed that spring and thrived with weekly letters after he left Minnesota. Lyle's first letters began in June 1941 with "Dear Marguerite" and were signed "Sincerely, Lyle". By August he was signing them "Love, Lyle". By October it was "Dearest Marguerite" and signed "I love you, Marguerite." Absence made our hearts grow fonder and my letters were equally affectionate, although he was only able to keep a few of mine …

* * * *

September 1941: *His letters described his job with the railroad.* "I've been doing a great variety of jobs in the first week. If it were not for the variety I'd probably be objecting to all the work rather than finding it interesting. Some of the jobs have been aligning railroad curves (checking to see if the elevation for the tracks are in the correct position to give smooth train riding), setting stakes from which the elevation of the tracks are determined, and running a level taking numbers off a few thousand rails and recording them, calculating in the office, filing papers, drawing maps, and acting as a clerk answering the telephone in the office. Today I got a long list of things to study and learn … six books which have to be known perfectly. Also there are things I have to learn by observation such as operation of machines and procedures in taking care of wrecks. I'm subject to calls anytime day or night."

* * * *

September 1941: "I received a blank from my draft board Monday. I've been deferred until December. If I want further deferment I must have my employer fill out a blank saying I'm working in an essential position in an essential industry. The railroad has not yet adopted a policy of asking deferments for any of their employees. Of course, being in the army wouldn't be so terribly bad, but I think I can be of more value where I am. The railroads are working full blast to get the raw products and finished materials to the places of greatest need. My department is essential to keep the track in condition for heavy traffic."

* * * *

October, 1941: *Lyle received a letter from his draft board instructing him to take his physical exam soon.* "I'm afraid I'll pass. They haven't acted on my deferment yet so I'm still hoping, though hopes are dimming. If I get drafted my dreams for the future will be smashed. Somehow you seem to dominate my dreams. That's why I'd hate to have my future postponed, so to speak."

* * * *

After Armistice Day in November 1941: *Lyle took his physical exam and passed* "in spite of a bad hangnail."

* * * *

After Pearl Harbor, December 7, 1941: *Lyle's letters did not mention Pearl Harbor specifically, but in December he wrote,* "The war is kind of hard to take. But now that we're in it we'll have to do our very best. I expect that before long we'll be fighting Germany and Italy too. Maybe by the time you read this. Sunday *(probably December 7th)* was a busy day for us to set up watchmen on all the railroad bridges and had a watchman on every mile of railroad. By Sunday night we were taking every precaution to guard against sabotage. The army has sentries on all the main highway bridges.

"I had to take a written examination on all I'm supposed to have learned so far. I wrote 23 pages and was told I did ok."

* * * *

Before Christmas 1941: "I received notice from my draft board that I am 1-A, and that they have declined all occupational deferments. I just got through filling out my application for a commission as a designer in the Air Corps. If I'm going I may as well try to get an officer's job."

Lyle came home to visit his parents in Granite Falls, Minnesota for Christmas, at which time we became engaged. It was a happy time for both of us and of our families. By New Year's Eve Lyle was back in Pittsburgh. Lyle had heard no more from his draft board. "I found out about a Railroad Operating Corps in the army which is offering a 2nd Lieutenant Commission. I've applied for that."

1942

January 6, 1942: *Postcard.* "I've been transferred. I am shuffling off to Buffalo, New York. Will write you as soon as I'm settled and can give you a new address."

His new address was in another rooming house: 149 Highland Avenue in Buffalo. He liked his work. "Here I'm treated with respect. I've my own desk and telephone and bigger responsibility. All the railroad men call me 'Assistant Supervisor' although that is not my title."

Back in Granite Falls, Lyle's dad wrote that two men he had working in the filling station and one in the lunchroom were taking defense jobs. Another was being drafted.

Lyle got "hooked" into singing in a barbershop quartet and went to church regularly with young men from his rooming house. At work he was assigned the extra task of getting Red Cross contributions from everyone, even contributed ten dollars himself.

Still trying to get a commission, Lyle applied to the naval ordnance department for work which involved land duty along engineering lines.

There was lots of snow in Buffalo. Lyle sometimes worked 26-30 hours straight. "Hired 370 men to help fight snow and spent $6000 yesterday just trying to keep the railroad operating. With all the defense traffic they insist that we keep things open and moving."

Later Lyle wrote, "I worked 18 hours yesterday without stopping once. My boss is in the hospital for a month so me being next in line I'm more or less in full charge of our subdivision." It was a battle with the snow in the winter and come spring, floods which washed out railroad beds. "Yesterday noon 2000 feet of railroad washed out."

* * * *

March 1942: *In March Lyle took his physical for engineering training in the Army Air Corps.* "I had the same examination as for the flying cadets, which really is tough. It took practically all day. Now unless something unforeseen turns up I will probably get an appointment as a cadet in a month or two. Then after 6 or 7 months if everything is satisfactory I will be a 2nd Lieutenant."

Not leaving any opportunity aside, Lyle applied for a job as a structural engineer with Curtis Wright Corporation, the largest manufacturer of airplanes in the country.

* * * *

April 22, 1942: *Lyle was in Granite Falls awaiting the draft. His mother invited my family for dinner, the first time our families had formally been together.*

I was a senior at the University of Minnesota and had loaded myself down with 19 credit hours, many more than I needed for graduation. Lyle worked for his dad during the week and came to see me every weekend. He spent many an hour waiting for me to finish typing a term paper before being free to spend time with him.

* * * *

May, 1942: *Lyle wrote from Granite Falls,* "I got a call from the draft this morning. I will go June 11th. That leaves us three more wonderful weekends together. I plan to come to the cities again on Friday for the weekend."

I graduated from the university in June and went home to the family farm in Dawson, Minnesota, for the summer, having accepted a position teaching sixth grade in Watervliet, Michigan, starting in September. Lyle knew he would be off in the army and agreed with my decision.

* * * *

June 26, 1942: *Receiving Company #3, Reception Center, Ft. Snelling, Minnesota. Lyle was assigned to Headquarters as a runner, running errands for everyone.* "It's better than KP," *he wrote.*

* * * *

July 4, 1942: "I got a letter from Washington saying that my appointment has been granted. I am to start training with a class beginning August 17th."

This was the cadet class for officer's training in the Army Air Corps. In the meantime he would stay at Ft. Snelling as a private.

One day while sitting outside the Headquarter' office Lyle overheard officers complain, "We don't even have a decent map of this place." *Lyle poked his head in the door,* "Sir, I heard what you said. I am a civil engineer. I can make a map for you." *Being in the right place at the right time …*

* * * *

July 22, 1942: "I finally got started on my map. Yesterday I surveyed all day and today I computed the results of yesterday's work. Tomorrow I'll be out in the field again. I've got swell instruments to work with which makes the job more enjoyable."

His letters referred to weekend bus trips or sometimes, hitchhiking to Granite Falls. We saw each other at those times as Granite Falls was only thirty miles from Dawson. Sometimes the passes were for three or four days. He finished the map.

* * * *

Chanute Field, Rantoul, Illinois
November 1942

Marching in mass formation

Old Glory Leading

Cadet Lyle Young

The new Mrs. Lyle Young

Now it's Lieutenant Lyle Young

August 24, 1942: *Aviation Cadet Detachment, Class 42-67, Bks. T-315, Chanute Field, Illinois.* "It's come through. I am now Aviation Cadet (A/C), not a Private. I was notified at 4 p.m. Friday to be ready at 6 p.m. I traveled first class to Chicago and then by coach via Illinois Central RR to Rantoul, Illinois. Spent yesterday afternoon enrolling in classes and getting new uniforms. I found that the training period has been cut from nine months to four and one-half months after which time we'll be commissioned either a 2nd Lieutenant or a Warrant Officer. After three weeks we'll be allowed a pass from 2 p.m. Saturday until 7 p.m. Sunday with a 20 mile limit except for once a month when we will be allowed a radius of 200 miles. I'm not sure if Watervliet is within that radius or not."

* * * *

August 26, 1942: "Following is a typical day. We are awakened at 4:30 a.m. We dress, make our beds, dust the room, etc., and line up on the road by 5:10. We march to breakfast in formation. (We never go anywhere unless we march in formation to and from classes, meals, etc.) We eat cafeteria style. Table manners are very strict. We stand until the table is filled and sit only when the last man calls 'seats' and eat only when he calls 'rest'. We must eat with our left hand in our laps at all times. We wait until all are done or ask to be excused. There are usually upper class men at each table and they must all be addressed as 'Sir'. We are addressed as 'Mister'. After breakfast we march to class which begins at 6.00. Classes have been rather tough because a few of us were a couple days late and had to catch up.

"Classes last until 11:45 when we march to dinner. From dinner we go back to class until 2:00. After class we march to barracks and put on dress uniforms taking off the overalls we wear to classes. We then spend until 5 p.m. drilling, calisthenics, and lectures. At 5 p.m. we march to supper and after supper we march 6 blocks back to barracks and then have until 7 p.m. free … between 7 and 9:30 we have to scrub the barracks and straighten lockers. Every piece of clothing has a special way to be folded or hung. For any small violation of neatness or rules we are awarded 'gigs' which are a demerit. We are allowed 4 gigs a week after which we must walk post one hour for each additional gig. I haven't any yet.

"I like it. We have a great deal of respect and have a crack outfit with marvelous spirit." *As always he closed with expressions of love for me and plans for the future.*

* * * *

August 29, 1942: *Lyle found he could get a three-day pass over Labor Day and that Watervliet was within the 200 mile limit. He asked me to meet him at the Illinois Central Station in Chicago on Saturday night and that he would like to go with me to Watervliet.* "Those passes are really in demand and it won't be often or ever we'll have Monday off too."

It all worked out. I met him in Chicago and we took a bus to Watervliet. I already had a place to stay and Lyle found a place. We talked and talked and decided to be married as soon as Lyle could get another weekend pass. Many of the cadets were married and had wives living near the base. Lyle wrote to both our parents to tell them of our plans and get their consent. I talked with my principal, Mr. Crocker, about our plans to marry and continue teaching.

Lyle suggested we be married in Champaign, Illinois because of his short passes (it was just 18 miles from Chanute Field in Rantoul, IL.). So many details … blood tests … the license. He suggested October 3rd. He needed to find a minister. Who would be our attendants? We didn't think our folks could come because of gas rationing. My roommate, Jean Pletcher, would be my bridesmaid and a cadet friend, Vic Smith from Colorado would be Lyle's best man. Lyle found Rev. Dwight P. Bair to marry us at the English Lutheran Church in Champaign, Illinois.

* * * *

October 3, 1942: *Our parents rode together for the wedding—nearly 700 miles. Lyle's father was able to get extra gas ration tickets from his customers who did not use all of theirs. My sister, Elizabeth Ann, came along to be my bridesmaid. My mother carried a wedding cake on her lap the entire trip. Other than our parents, Jean Pletcher and her boyfriend and some of Lyle's cadet friends from Chanute Field were our only wedding guests. As many wartime ready-made clothes were sleazy, and knowing how to sew, I bought maroon-colored velveteen and a Vogue pattern to make my own two-piece wedding dress—on my landlady's sewing machine.*

We were married at 4 p.m., and had our wedding picture taken at a studio on the way to the hotel. My parents hosted a dinner for all the wedding guests at the Tilden Hotel. The next morning our parents and my sister started their return trip to Minnesota and that afternoon I had to take a train back to Watervliet, and Lyle returned to Chanute Field.

According to Lyle's letters I met him in Champaign for the next two weekends. He came to Watervliet the last weekend in October. Wonderful, precious weekends for us newlyweds …

* * * *

November 5, 1942: "From now on Thursday is my day off and I have to go to school on Sunday. Some big shot thinks we're having it too soft. We can plan on Thanksgiving anyway. That is all in sight for now." *We wrote letters every day ...*

* * * *

November 10, 1942: "What would you think of quitting your job at Christmas vacation and going with me wherever I'm sent? Perhaps you could get a leave of absence for a couple of months and go back to Watervliet when I go overseas."

Lyle had classes in airplane maintenance, military law, chemical warfare; he ordered officer uniforms, dark green shirt and pants, grey pants, a tan trench coat, officer's hat and three pair of bars, a belt and necktie. All for $69.50, but $80.00 less than his $150 uniform allowance. Later when the uniform allowance was increased he ordered the dark green officer's dress blouse. He wrote, "I got a gig for dust on a little ledge that the drawer of our table slides on. Who'd ever expect anyone to look under a table for dust?

"In administration class today I learned that as a 2nd Lieutenant we get $150 base pay plus $21 for you and $21 for me for subsistence and $60 per month for quarters or quarters on a base. We will be able to live very nicely on that and probably save money. I get free transportation and a free trip for you one way only. Tomorrow we appear before a board of officers to determine if we are suitable for officers. I'm not worried because my record is good."

* * * *

November 26, 1942: *We spent Thanksgiving weekend at the base, very happy to be together. I did talk to Mr. Crocker about resigning at Christmas vacation, and Lyle and I made plans for the holiday. He got two days off at Christmas and two days off at New Year's.*

* * * *

Holidays, 1942: *Between Christmas and New Year's Lyle made arrangements for me to take the train to Minnesota to see our families. Afterwards, Lyle and his friend, Onnie Wooten, rented rooms for the two couples at a house near the University of Illinois campus. Onnie and Lyle drew straws and Onnie and Sarah got the larger room. Lyle and I had a bedroom with no closet or dresser drawer space. Everything was full, even under the bed. We only needed the rooms for a short time until the men got their commissions, so we made do. My steamer trunk stood in the hallway near our* *shared bathroom. (These may have been rooms usually lived in by students, off on Christmas break.)*

1943

January 9, 1943: *The men were commissioned and had orders immediately to report to Key Field at Meridian, Mississippi. Sarah and Onnie Wooten grew up in Senatobia, Mississippi, and invited us to spend one night at the Wooten family home, en route to the men's new assignments.*

Lyle remembers very little about his work. They were forming an outfit of men with a few officers and a 1st Sergeant. Soldiers were sent to them. The outfit received tools which they waterproofed with cosmoline. Boxes were made to hold the tools and equipment and had to be floatable in the event boxes were thrown overboard into the ocean during landings. Lyle doesn't ever remember seeing those boxes again, but the work kept them busy. By the time they were ready to leave Waycross the unit had 230 men and five officers: Commander, Supply, Engineering, Medical, and Adjutant. Sometimes Lyle was both Supply and Engineering Officer.

According to Lyle, the tricky part about Supply was anticipating and ordering the specific parts for airplanes. The men did not do a lot of work on airplanes until they got to Dobadura, New Guinea. Then they had a full operation.

We spent the next six months on Lyle's short assignments at Key Field in Meridian, Venice Air Base at Venice, Florida, and lastly at Waycross Air Base at Waycross, Georgia. We always lived off base. The transition from Minnesota to the South was a culture shock, yet those were happy months because we were together. We did not have a car. Lyle got rides to the bases with friends. I walked a lot. We enjoyed socializing with other officers and their wives, and made new friends. Everything was tentative. We did not know how long we would be at any one base. As the pictures show, perhaps a couple of months, and then our men would be going overseas—somewhere.

Venice, Florida, was just a village in 1943. Housing was very scarce, and we lived a short time at a hotel, the Villa Nokomis, which did not serve meals. It had quit serving meals because there were no tourists. So I bought cans of tomato juice and crackers to have in our room—a good choice for a newly pregnant girl. In the evening Lyle and I walked along a grapefruit orchard on our way to the village to find a restaurant. We did not have much money, and I recall that omelets were a frequent choice. I loved the fresh grapefruit and oranges.

A week or so later, Lyle found a little house for us on Venice Inlet. We were right on the shore of the Gulf of Mexico. The sun shone all day, and the palm trees blew. I did my own laundry, and hung it on lines but things did not really dry because the air was so humid. Dampness brought mildew. When we turned lights on at night, strange insects scurried across the floors. And faucet water tasted like sulfur, so we bought our drinking water. But we could walk to the beach and see ships in a distance. We walked on the jetty to watch porpoises dance in and out of the water. How delightful. We enjoyed living in each new community. Many decades later, we visited Venice, and tried to find our old location. But the village had become a large city.

Then Waycross, Georgia. We knew Lyle would soon be shipped out. Across from our large house (we had an upstairs apartment) was a park. On some nights we heard soldiers practicing their marching to a wonderful rhythm. We could never fully escape the knowledge that we would be parted too soon …

Lt. Lyle Young and wife Margie's First Homes

Our first apartment was in Meridian, Mississippi from January to March 1943

Our second home was a cottage at Venice Inlet at Venice, Florida, on the Gulf of Mexico. The beach was our front yard. The street was downtown Venice. March and April, 1943.

Our third home was at 905 Mary St. in Waycross, Georgia, from May to June 1943. It was an upstairs apartment in this home.

June 28, 1943: *Lyle wrote to me from Waycross after putting me on a train back to Minnesota to live with my parents on the farm for the duration of the war. It was good we did not know that more than two years would pass before we would be together again. I was pregnant. Lyle wrote,* "In spite of the fact we parted with only a few tears it was the hardest thing I've ever had to do … how we kept so cheerful those last few days I'll never know, but I'm glad it was that way." *I remember crying myself to sleep in my berth on the train. We had had six wonderful months together since Christmas.*

Lyle wrote that he was living in a room in the Bachelor Officer Quarters (BOQ) with Capt. Bundschuh and that they got along swell. "I'm Engineering Officer now, the job I want. It calls for Capt., but I'll have to serve my required time before I can get that. Hope to get my silver bars (1st Lieutenant) soon.

"We've been busy. I've been teaching classes in tactics, have so little knowledge of the subject I've managed to keep just one step ahead of the men by reading Manuals on the different subjects. I've taught Chemical Warfare, Camouflage, Field Sanitation, First Aid, Security and Defense measures, Hand Signals, Care and Shooting of Rifles and Machine Guns. Also Jungle Fighting and Methods of the Japanese Army. Tomorrow I'm going to work on Arctic Warfare. I wish I had some infantry experience to help me put this across better. The men are patient though and are very interested in the subjects so I get by. I'm hoarse now from talking most of the day."

Another letter came from Waycross. "Tonight we're getting ready to go out on bivouac again. We're going to wake the men at 4 a.m. tomorrow morning, break camp in the dark and move out. We're going about fifteen miles from here to camp and coming back Sunday." *After they returned, Lyle wrote,* "Our sham battle, or maneuvers, or whatever you want to call it worked out quite nicely. We made a lot of mistakes but that is what we expected. Now we're giving lectures and had discussions to correct the mistakes. It was hard work. The men came back in all wringing wet with perspiration and exhausted.

"In the *National Geographic* of June 1943, page 720, is a copy of our Squadron's exclusive insignia. We are one of the few Service Squadrons to have an approved insignia. We are a little proud of it.

"It has been terribly hot here for the last week, hotter than ever before this year. The walls of the B.O.Q. were hot all night. There is no breeze during the day at all. It is almost too hot to hike or do much work at all. I can easily see how the Southerners get lazy. Once in awhile, we get a little rain, which relieves the heat somewhat; but usually it gets hot quickly again. I hope to get out of this climate soon."

* * * *

July 25, 1943: *Lyle and his Squadron left for the South Pacific; left to see the war firsthand. They sailed unescorted on the USS Taft, a private passenger liner taken over by the government as a troop ship. Troop ships that sailed in a convoy sailed more slowly, while an unescorted ship could sail faster. The USS Taft served delicious meals in the elegant manner as in peacetime … at least to the officers. The officers bunked six men to a stateroom.*

It was a long voyage all the way to Townsville, on the northeastern coast of Australia. Lyle was given a mimeographed certificate called The Ancient Order of the Deep, certifying that he had been gathered into our fold and initiated as a Shellback, having crossed the equator and invaded my realm aboard the U.S.A.T. Willard A. Holbrook on August 2, 1943, at Latitude 00'00'. It was signed by Captain I. A. Pfieffer, Commanding Officer. (When the USS Taft became a troop ship it was give the new name.)

New Guinea 1943–44
100th Service Squadron Dobadura Air Base

Clearing out the jungle for their shop at Dobadura

Lyle Young at the Bamboo Inn, his home away from home.
They had thatching for the sides of the building until they got some burlap.
Their helmets were their wash-basins.

Staff Sergeant Riggs, Lieutenant Hook, Lieutenant Young
Members of the Engineering Office on Dobadura

January 2, 1944
Handsome New Guinea man wears armbands as a mark of his tribe

Natives pose for picture before their dance celebrating the Harvest Festival

August 19, 1943. Somewhere in Australia. *Lyle had not gotten any letters from me in a long time. They were paid in Australian money, and said that people lived simply and dressed accordingly.* "Their speech is a little hard to understand. The main dish of the Aussies seems to be steaks. A small steak costs about fifty cents, American money.

"We are living in tents and eating on mess kits. All my boyhood desires for camping out are satisfied."

* * * *

August 30, 1943. "Yesterday work slacked up a bit, so a couple of Lts. and I went kangaroo hunting. We saw a couple but didn't do much with our automatic pistols. The country around here is a lot like western U.S. There are a lot of cattle, and people use horses a lot."

* * * *

September 9, 1943. *Townsville was a staging area, and the Squadron stayed there about three weeks. Leaving all their equipment behind, they flew to Port Moresby on the south coast of New Guinea, another staging area. After a few days the Squadron flew over the Owen Stanley Mountains to Dobadura, near Buna. Our National Geographic Atlas and several other books on the Pacific campaign show Buna, but not Dobadura, perhaps because Dobadura was an airstrip, not a town.*

Lyle remembers some of the Aussie Scouts who traveled alone into the jungle carrying radios and living off the land. Their purpose was to climb the high lookouts from which they could observe the enemy activity and report back to the bases. These were dangerous missions, not only because of the jungle, but because their radio contacts could be picked up by the Japanese, making them vulnerable to capture or death.

Buna was in an almost impenetrable jungle, which had to be bulldozed out to establish the bases, and later, the landing strips, work and living areas at Dobadura. The 100th Service Squadron established their first major base at Dobadura. While the men flew in, their equipment arrived by LSTs. Then for eight months they remained at the base repairing and maintaining aircraft. There was lots of action from their planes to other points of New Guinea, in New Britain and the Admiralty Islands. The Squadron serviced P18s, B-24s, and B-25s.

Lyle began the next letter, "Dear Nora. We are so far apart. If I were to go in any direction, I don't think I could be any further away." *We had worked out a code to tell us where we were. N stood for New Guinea*

* * * *

September 17, 1943. "A darn good piece of news came the other day. I finally got my 1st Lt. promotion as of August 9th. That will increase my pay to $299.50 a month. Instead of taking a chance on things getting mixed up I'll just send home extra checks as the last check was $180. Now we can save a little more for the future."

"Mrs. Roosevelt spoke here the other day. She drove up in a big car with about 50 guards and spoke to us for about 15 minutes. She was dressed in the uniform of the Red Cross and looked nicer than her pictures. I think I got my mug in a picture." *(Interestingly, the date was cut out.)*

* * * *

October 3, 1943. "Today marks one year that we have been husband and wife. I only regret that I cannot be with you. Soon we will have the mark of a family, a baby … It is raining and the floor of the tent is rather muddy. What is it that mud baths are good for? I received the Sunday paper a few days ago, but I still haven't received the washing machine or the piano!" I don't need a grand piano, just an upright will do.

"It is getting toward summer here, and is already terribly hot. The south U.S. is like the dead of winter compared to this place. They tell me 130 degrees is not uncommon, although it hasn't gotten that hot yet. It will be a luxury to have sheets again, springs, and a pillow. But such is the army. We do get nourishing food though."

* * * *

October 18, 1943: *A.P.O. 503, Unit 1, c/o Postmaster, San Francisco, California.* "Notice the change of address. "Today I was out in the jungle with Warrant Officer (W.O.) Mr. Burkett chopping down some bamboo. We are going to try to get our tent up off the ground before the rainy season sets in. The jungle is very dense; one has to cut one's way through every foot of the way. It is full of all kinds of vegetation, insects, and birds imaginable. One of the men brought in an orchid that measured 13 inches in diameter. Imagine what a beautiful corsage that would make. There are parrots and many other birds that keep up a continuous chatter. The place we are in now isn't so bad. There is a river which has been cleared of crocodiles and is ok for swimming."

* * * *

October 25, 1943: "Still no mail. The men are all rather blue. The Captain, W.O. Mr. Burkett and I have almost finished our tent. We moved in the other day and are enjoying the luxury of a floor. We have a couple of boys working on a washing machine. It is made out of old oil barrels, scraps of iron and reinforcing rod. It is really four machines run by the same engine. It is designed with separate tubs for white and dark, and two for rinsing clothes." *(He included a sketch)*

* * * *

November 1, 1943: "We dickered with the natives and they thatched the sides of our tent about two feet around the bottom. It looks like a real native structure now. The natives are quite clever with their use of natural materials. They get broad leaves out of the jungle and make mats out of them by weaving and tying the leaves together with small vines. They then put the mats together and make huts. The huts are rainproof and cooler than other structures. The natives speak a crude kind of English which sounds like a mixture of pig Latin and baby talk. It is almost impossible to understand, but they understand plain English fairly well so we can tell them what we want even though they can't answer back.

"We are all getting yellow complexions from the yellow atabrine pills that we take to keep down malaria. It will go away when we quit taking the pills. We also take a daily vitamin tablet to supplement our diet which is lacking in fresh foods.

"I'm still waiting for news of the new arrival. You have told me not to worry, but I can't help but be anxious and impatient. To have a baby of our own, a part of us, will go toward making our home even happier than before, although that hardly seems possible." *Lyle was drawing house plans for the house we hope to build some day.* "I finally sent the house plans. Hope you like them … the color scheme will be entirely up to you.

"Did you ever receive the $170 I sent October 8th? Summarizing, I've sent $180 and $170, besides the allotments which were $150 up until October and then $250 for the first time this month. You've been doing very well saving, darling. That can go toward a house, furniture or a car when I get back. Don't deny yourself or the baby anything you need or want. Above all I want you to be well cared for.

"I was talking with a native the other day who could speak good English. He has great admiration for America and Americans. He said that he had seen many pictures of the beautiful buildings, roads, cars and trains in the U.S. and hoped to see them some day. He has never seen a white woman. I showed him your picture which I carry in my billfold and he said, 'Very good wife' and added, 'You lucky'. He's not the only one who knows that.

"As I write this there are about 30 natives building a grass hut in back of our tent. We are going to use the tent as a Day Room. They keep up a continual jabber. I've been trying to pick out the one who is the boss but they all seem to be pretty busy. They will leave every once in awhile to go into the jungle and bring out a pole, some leaves, grass and vines which they need in their construction. The building is going up amazingly fast, having risen since morning. You'd find them very interesting, I know. Wish you were here.

"I have to give a lecture tonight. We are still carrying on a limited training program to keep the men on their jobs. I am enclosing a couple of coins. The large one is a penny or pence and is worth one and one-third cents in our money. The small one is a half penny or as the Aussies call it a 'hapnee'. In writing monetary amounts they look something like this: 2f 6s 2 1/2d which is two pounds, 6 shillings, and 2 ½ pence. The use of money, like driving on the left side of the road, is perfectly natural now.

"We've been all working hard, long hours and putting out every effort to 'keep 'em flying'. I'm proud of my men and their ability to put out a lot of work and all precision too. We are still getting our daily swim. That is one of the best features of this place. After getting hot and dirty there is nothing like it. The stream is fast and clear and the banks are lined with dense jungle which almost covers over the top. The jungles are steaming hot.

"Last night Capt. B. and I went to a show in an Aussie camp. It was 'Stormy Weather' with an all Negro cast. I enjoyed it even though the sound wasn't so hot.

"You mention in a letter about the philosophies of the men changing due to the war. I think that a lot of the men will change. Those that have something stable like a wife and family will be the least affected. One day I wrote down my thoughts. Here they are: I am a censor. A censor has a job that gives him a hard look into the personal lives and thoughts of his men. Those personal bits are none of my business, yet they are there and must be read. Men resent another reading their correspondence until they realize it is first necessary for military reasons, and second, their personal affairs are not open to anyone but the censor. This duty has given me a better understanding of men. Outwardly a soldier may be anything: rough, cruel, hateful, kind, respectful, or mild, but inside there is the spark or flame of the good that is in all men. War's cruelty makes men act in ways unnatural. We did not choose this war. We accept it and put every effort into it because without it we would lose the life that every man wants. The men know what they are fighting for. There are political reasons, but the real reason is to assure that the life they left, the life they want to live, can be theirs. The army has brought to its soldiers a better under-standing of men. Most of these men have two characters: the outward one which is apparent and the inner character which appears only after long and close contact with the men. Basically, they are all pretty much the same. They are fighting and toiling for the purposes they know are right. The purposes vary with each man, but basically they all add up to the right to live, worship, and work in peace. Each man has constant dreams of home, his loved ones, the neat little house, the neighbors, the church. He now realizes that those are the most important things in life and without them there is nothing. Through sweat and blood the vision of an honest world grows brighter."

As a censor, Lyle once came upon an awkward situation: a soldier had written his wife and *his mistress, but had mistakenly switched the letters in the envelopes. Lyle realized the man's mistake, but decided to let it stand and sent them off… part of his philosophy of "an honest world."*

* * * *

November 19, 1943: "Very little uncensorable news. Things are running smoothly and life has settled down to a routine. Get up at 5:45, eat breakfast and start work at 7. I start off the day by censoring mail and after that take off in my jeep to visit various departments and see if everything is going ok, or if department heads need anything. We have chow at noon which consists of different concoctions of corned beef, dehydrated potatoes, a canned vegetable, sometimes fruit, and bread without butter. After dinner I make my rounds again and do anything else that comes up. In the evening about 6:00 I drive down to the river and wash my jeep, clothes, and yours truly which have all gotten filthy from the dusty roads. The roads are the roughest things imaginable and one gets jolted around quite a bit. Supper, hash and beans and then in the evenings I write a letter first and then read, go to a show, or just talk. Rather a dull life except for your letters which I read over and over again.

"The food has improved a bit lately. The cooks are discovering new ways of fixing bully beef every day. We have it baked, in hash, broiled, in sandwiches, fried in hamburger fashion, and just plain cold. The cooks do a swell job of making tasty dishes. About once a week we have fresh meat and about once a month fresh eggs, which help a lot.

"Gotta give a lecture tonight at 7 p.m. so have been getting material together. Guess I shoulda been a teacher. Another of those 'in addition to your other duties' that the army has so many of." *After the war, Lyle became a teacher—a professor in Engineering at the University of Minnesota and then the University of Nebraska, where he also became Associate Dean of Engineering, and served as Interim Dean for two years.*

* * * *

November 23, 1943: "Somewhere in New Guinea. No, I haven't moved, the censorship rules have loosened up a little. Am sending you another picture. You'll have to be a little broad-minded about this one. The couple is nicer looking than the average. Most natives have a wild look and are ugly. Women are scarce. This picture was taken at the native village a few miles from here.

"I'm a little tired tonight. I got up at 2 a.m. to get some trucks we need. It was rather hard to make the 20 men I took with me realize that getting up that early was worth getting 11 trucks."

* * * *

November 25, 1943: "Today is Thanksgiving. We had a nice dinner with turkey, etc. It was not up to home cooked standards but it was a real treat. The biggest treat was a real genuine ice cube. That was the first cold drink I've had in several months. One really misses such little things. We had work as usual today. We can't let down just because of holidays."

* * * *

November 29, 1943: "At last I just received your V-mail of November 10th. I'm so very happy. It will take me awhile to really realize that it is true just as it did after we were married. The name is lovely. Lois Marie, very sweet, feminine, and simple. She is a very big baby ... I'd give anything to see her. I'll bet she is very cute. You must send a picture as soon as you can ... one of you too, darling. I will have to go out to work now. I'll stick my chest out and hold my growing head high and be the proudest father that ever was." *Lois Marie was born November 9th, 1943 and weighed over ten pounds.*

* * * *

November 30, 1943: "The little hand and foot prints were very cute. They are so little and delicate, but also very nicely shaped. The more I think of the name Lois Marie the more I like it. It is a swell choice. The idea of using our initials is clever. You ask about godparents. You suggested Gordon and Jean and that would be fine." *My brother and Lyle's sister.*

* * * *

December 1, 1943: "Censorship regulations have let up a little now so I can tell you of some news from time to time. We are in close contact with planes that bomb Wewak, Raboul, Madang, and others. We see them leave on missions and wait for their return. We prepare the planes for the next mission. That is our job: to fix any damage and inspect for wear. We get first hand information from returning pilots and invariably news is good. The Nip losses in ships, planes, and ground installations are terrific, but they are stubborn little devils and really have to be bombed out completely.

"I saw about fifty Jap Zeros raid here one day; our planes and ack ack knocked down 44 of them. It was quite a spectacle to watch, although I couldn't see too well from the slit trench. The Japs are terribly inaccurate. It seems they never hit anything. They don't come around much anymore."

Their base at Dobadura was frequently attacked in the daytime, so men had to go to the slit trenches for safety. He doesn't remember losing any of their men.

"Yesterday we held a citation ceremony. We thought it up and run it off in a very military manner. There was a long address. It ended up by pinning a pair of wings with JEEP PILOT painted on them and an aluminum cross on one of our boys who drives a little fast. He was cited for his ability to get over any object and his proficiency in buzzing the area, and was complimented on the way he drove larger vehicles with the same reckless abandon. It went off very well and everyone almost split to keep from laughing (we were at attention). It was unexpected by the men and they really got a big kick out of it. Several told me it was the funniest thing they have seen in a long time.

"We've been enjoying 130 degree weather for the last few days. It is rough to be out in the sun very long. It has been raining a lot too. The nights have been moderately cool so that helps for sleeping. Our mosquito nets cut off some of the breeze."

* * * *

December 3, 1943: "I got a letter from the folks today. They are very proud grandparents and think Lois Marie a very lovely baby. I'm so anxious to see her." *He would not see her until she had had her second birthday …*

* * * *

December 6, 1943: "Our planes have been taking a heavy toll of Jap shipping, barges, and planes. We've been doing our part in keeping 'em flying. The men have been doing exceptional work and our organization has already developed a good reputation. We see the planes as they go out on raids and watch them come in. Then the crew gives us the results of the raids which are invariably good. The Japs cannot come up to either our men or equipment standards. They are stubborn though and far from beaten.

"I have read your letter no less than six times since it came this morning. Your letters are so important in keeping my chin up. I eagerly look forward to them and read them over and over again so as not to miss any thought. Realizing how important letters are to me, I have been writing to you every day.

"Capt. B. and I are building a shower in back of our tent. We've got an old tank and some scraps from an airplane and a few boards and some old burlap sacks. It will look like this. *(Sketch enclosed).* It is surprising what can be made out of old junk. Just a pile of pipes, etc., can be made into some handy things. I've made plans for some other things so the men can make them."

* * * *

December 11, 1943: "We are having more rain than I've ever seen before. It rained all afternoon. Our tent leaks in several spots and my bed is wet. There is a spot over it that I can't seem to waterproof. I'm glad we have floors in our tent because there are 6 inches of water all over outside. The soil is sandy about a foot under so the water will soak up in a day or so after it quits. It rains so hard that it fills up my steel helmet in about one-half hour. The helmet sits outside and I use it as a wash basin. Our slit trench is full of water too, I see. I hope Tojo doesn't bother us tonight. A lot of us got soaked that way one night.

"Our planes are completing a lot of successful missions. They are destroying a lot of the Nips' planes, boats and ground installations with negligible loss. Before I got here I thought our papers printed exaggerated claims, but now I find they are accurate. We are getting many compliments and encouraging reports on our work. I am proud of my men."

* * * *

December 12, 1943: "I just finished reading *Guinea Gold (newspaper).* The news looks encouraging. The Nazi party is crumbling. We are anxiously awaiting the end of the European war so those boys can give us a hand to clean up the Japs as soon as possible. Things move slowly though so it might take some time. The supply problem is enormous. A splendid job is being done.

"There is so little I can tell you. Our work has developed into somewhat a routine although it is far from monotonous. We have the same general type of work each day, but new and interesting technical problems are always coming up. Then there are firsthand accounts of action each day to keep interest up. I can without exaggeration say that we have the best setup in this theater of operations. Our work is high in quality and quantity. I'm proud of the organization. My men have backed me all the way.

"I was down on the beach today. It reminds me of Venice. *(Florida)* That was a pleasant place. Remember the problems of getting meals at the Villa Nokomis, the long walks and then the inlet with the swimming, walks on the jetty, time with the Erratts, reading *Kitty Foyle*, the awful water, and financial troubles. I do a lot of remembering now.

"Tonight we are going to have a show, *Pride of the Yankees*, which I've already seen twice. You can never tell though, I might have missed a couple of details so I'll go again. We have some logs laid on the ground for seats.

"Work goes on as usual. The most interesting part of the day is when planes return from a raid. They will come in and buzz the field; dive down to a few feet off the ground and go by the operations tower at full speed. Then as they swoop up they will flip over. This movement indicates the enemy planes shot down and is called a Victory Roll. Often a plane will take two Victory Rolls indicating a successful day. I've had the opportunity to go along on a few bombing missions, but will always refrain from taking any unnecessary chances. I've a big responsibility of a wife and daughter that I love and will come back to.

"I'm sorry that I didn't write last evening, but I was working and couldn't squeeze in the time. That's the first day I've missed in a long time. I haven't heard from you in a week now. Have you been writing regularly? I'm sorry, I know you have, it's just the irregularity of the mail. Today (Dec. 16) I got a letter from Jean *(his sister)* dated Nov. 2nd and the last letter from you about a week ago was dated Nov. 28th, so you can see how mixed up things are.

"Tonight the chaplain was over for supper. He is a Lutheran from Kansas. Right now he's watching a ball game. We have several teams in the Squadron and a couple of them play almost every evening. After the game we are going to have church services in the mess hall. Lately we've had the opportunity to go to church quite often which is a good thing. A man over here more than ever needs spiritual guidance."

* * * *

December 20, 1943: "The mail has been more regular the last three days. Your letters of November 27, 28, 29, 30th and Dec.1st have arrived. Darling, you are writing every day too. It is really the only way. Letters are such a big comfort. They are all I have to bring me close to you now except your picture."

* * * *

December 23, 1943: "What does this date suggest? It was just two years ago tonight that I became the world's luckiest man ... the question with the answer that brought us to belong to each other. We both were so happy as we drove out to the farm. You insisted on waking your folks to show them the ring and tell them the news."

* * * *

December 24, 1943: "Here it is Christmas Eve. A couple nights ago the chaplain came over with his portable organ and we had a Christmas carol sing in the mess hall. We sang every song we would think of, with gusto. The program went so well that the men suggested a weekly sing fest for the Squadron. Schilling and I hope to organize some kind of men's choir. We have a lot of good voices in the Squadron.

"My mind goes back to previous years. I remember all the years of childhood when we looked forward in anxious anticipation to this evening of the year. The whole family would pitch in and help with supper dishes so that we could start the festivities. As children we always had to give a program. We'd sing or recite the little verse that we had to give at the church program. Sometimes they'd be done rather hurriedly because we'd want to open that box with the funny rattling noise that we were so curious about. Each would open their gifts and then we'd arrange them and admire each one and express our thanks. It was wonderfully cozy and peaceful. Tonight I have the gifts I've received before me and am trying to get up a little spirit but without much success.

"Last year we had Christmas Eve at the Boise's *(the name of the people who owned a house with the rooms Wootens and we had rented).* We were together, that was our biggest gift. Our next Christmas together will be the best of all …" *That would not be until Christmas 1945 …* "Now we have Lois to share it with. Children are really necessary to get full enjoyment out of Christmas."

* * * *

December 25, 1943: "You have made my Christmas happy with your two letters which came through today. They were swell letters full of memories of the past, of Lois Marie, of the future, and prayers for the future. We had a nice Christmas dinner today. Last night after I finished my letter to you I went over to the mess hall and spent the evening decorating it with palm leaves and shrubbery. There are no plants like evergreens here so it didn't look much like Christmas, but I think everyone got the general idea. We had chicken for dinner. A boat arrived at the last moment with supplies. The men enjoyed the noon hour very much. It wasn't like Christmas dinners we had at home with more kinds of food than one could possibly eat. It was nice though and well-prepared. The cooks stayed up all night and their efforts were appreciated."

* * * *

December 27, 1943: "Today I made an inventory of the PX. It is one of those 'in addition to your other duties' jobs which a man catches occasionally. The PXs over here don't amount to much. They will get two or three items and sell them all the first hour that they open. Men will buy things they don't even need just to get the feel of spending money again. Soap is a main item of exchange.

"Our candle light service last night was quite impressive. We put up about 100 candles and they were the only light. Each man came forward and took communion holding a candle. I didn't know such a reverent atmosphere could be held in New Guinea.

"There has been a fine dust settling on everything the last couple of days. Today I learned it is volcanic ash from a volcanic eruption a long way off somewhere.

"The marines, army, navy, and Australian diggers as Australians call their soldiers, are doing a splendid job of fighting under tremendous difficulties of jungle terrain and heat. You cannot imagine how cruel the jungles are until you have been in them. The air force has now reached a strength which allows us daily bombing and strafing raids on several enemy strongholds. The Nip is definitely going backwards up the road to Tokyo. It isn't a question of who will win, but simply when."

* * * *

December 31, 1943: "Happy New Year, darling. 1943 has really been an eventful year. In it we have enjoyed all the happiness of our marriage and the sorrow of being apart. It started well with graduation from cadets and travel to Meridian. There we had the thrill of setting up our own little home for the first time. It was a cozy apartment and we were happy there. We also enjoyed the companionship of Sarah and O.B. Those evenings spent listening to the radio, having colas, planning, etc., are among my fondest memories. We had our trip home in March. The most outstanding of that was the *(bridal)* shower we were given … the kindness and friendship in back of it all.

"Venice was a vacation paradise, but a housing nightmare. We made the best of it. It was a hardship for you, but you took it like the sport you always were. Finally, we got our little cottage on Venice inlet; then life was more enjoyable.

"Then Waycross where we sweated out the time until we knew we would have to part. We would have enjoyed the stay more if we had not had to dread that day which came on June 25th. That was the saddest day I've ever had. We kept our emotions under control admirably, but it was hard.

"I have mentioned hardships and trials, but really they were nothing as long as we were together. Think, darling, of the days ahead together with no thought of parting to interrupt our married bliss."

So ended 1943. Lyle was still at Dobadura in New Guinea. Since leaving the States he had been briefly in Townsville, Australia, then in New Guinea with brief stays at Port Moresby before flying over the Owen Stanley Mountains to Dobadura for an extended duty.

But it was not over yet …

1944

January 2, 1944. "Today we witnessed the natives holding some kind of celebration. Most of the morning, they had contests in throwing spears, shooting arrows, running and other sports. This afternoon was the big dance. The men were dressed in their finest splendor. They wore big bonnets made out of feathers, shells, and bones … ornaments on their ears, noses, arms and legs … their faces painted orange or white. The women and children watched and sometimes joined in the dance. Each man carried a tom-tom made out of a hollow log with a snakeskin stretched over it. As they danced, they beat out a weird rhythm and chant … there must have been a couple thousand of them. The native police and Aussies kept order."

* * * *

January 4, 1944. "On one night a week we are going to have a bingo party in the mess hall. The men buy three cards for two bob (a florine) and the winner takes all. It doesn't present a very exciting evening, but over here entertainment doesn't have to be much to be enjoyed. We get rained out of quite a few shows. Our theater is just two poles with a cloth stretched across for a screen, and a box to set the projector on. Everyone brings his own box to sit on. Our screen is so thin that we can sit on both sides of it. On the back, the picture is reversed, of course … The Aussies come to all our shows.

"The Aussies are a fine bunch of men. They are hardy and likeable … There are quite a few boys who married Australian girls while stationed in Australia … There are many 'diggers' who want to see the U.S. after the war, and a lot of Yanks who want to see Australia."

* * * *

January 6, 1944. "Today I was on a courts martial We had three trials to act upon. In the army, men are tried by a courts martial consisting of one to seven men depending on the seriousness of the charge. I was on the C. M. of four members who have the same function as judge and jury in a civilian court. The Articles of War are the law set up by the U.S. Congress. There is a defense and prosecution council just as civilian courts. I can't tell the details of these cases. It was a good experience. I'd had a course in military law, but this was the first time I'd put my knowledge to work."

* * * *

January 29, 1944: "Today the pictures came in your letter. They are wonderful. I've looked forward to them for so long. Our daughter is even more beautiful than I'd imagined. Those big innocent eyes, that chubby little face and hands are lovely. The picture of you, darling is very good—I will treasure these pictures along with the ones I have of you from before.

"My, our bank account is really growing. Today is the end of another month. It is just one more towards the time when I can come back to you and Lois. Each day sees us a little closer to victory. Some progress is being made on all fronts. I'm still hoping for the last part of this year. It will hardly be before then unless I was evacuated for sickness or something and I'd rather not go that way. It has been seven months and six days since that sad night in Waycross when we parted. It has seemed much longer … it will not take a great deal to fulfill our desires. Simply being together will take care of everything.

"I got paid today 6f 5'3d. I've had a few more expenses this month. Envelopes, shoes, postage, all add up. Just about all my suntans are worn out. I'll have to buy some new ones soon. Textiles rot in no time over here.

"The only thing that could make this place cheerful tonight is you. It is dark and dreary. The rain is pouring down outside and dripping inside the tent in places. I'm all alone; everyone having gone somewhere and there are no lights except a small piece of candle. I'll go to bed early, but the bed is damp too. It is a contrast to a cold winter night at home with a nice clean dry bed with sheets and a pillow, and best of all you to cuddle up to.

"Today my Aussie friend, Lt. Boun came over. It didn't take much to convince him to stay for supper, or tea, as he calls it. It seems that they receive pretty much the same rations as we, but our cooks do a better job of preparing the food. He's been here a couple of times and seems to enjoy the meals a lot. He eats in the typical English way with his fork in his left hand at all times and the right hand free for using the knife. I gave him a little tobacco which he was happy to get. The

American tobacco is very superior to Aussie brands; the Aussie really go for our product.

"So the little darling has taken to sucking her thumb. Shame, Lois. You must make every effort to stop her before she gets the habit—I'm not much of an authority on such things. To stop her you might make a little cloth covering for her thumb and tie it on like a bandage. I've seen it work.

"Did I tell you that we have a rumor board on which the men pin up the latest rumor. Today I put in my two cents worth: 'All members of this command of the rank of Private to Captain inclusive will upon completion of one year's service (bad time not included) in the South West theater of operations, automatically begin their second year of service'.

"Today we had some roast pork, imagine! I guess some boat just got here by mistake. That's the first time I've tasted pork in seven months. I've not had a glass of milk in that time either and probably won't until we get back through the Golden Gate.

"I've been doing quite a bit of reading. I just read *Report from Tokyo* by Joseph Grew, our former Ambassador to Japan. He tells of the preparations that were made prior to Pearl Harbor—quite interesting. Also read a couple mysteries again. We don't get much else over here. I read until I get all the clues and try to solve the thing before the author gives the solution."

* * * *

February 6, 1944: "Your V-mail letter of January 25th came today. That's just 12 days. V-mail comes through quicker than air mail but I'd rather receive air mail because they are longer and somehow more personal.

"I'm waiting for the bugle to blow church call. We just finished a ball game. I didn't realize it was Sunday until a little while ago. Every day is the same over here. Holidays are unheard of. It is the only way of course. It gives us 52 extra days a year to get our job done. The tempo of the war is speeding up all the time in all theaters of operation. The climax, particularly in Europe, should come before long. Things do look encouraging, and I'm still hoping to make it home in 1944:" *He would not get home until late 1945.*

"Does anyone around home ever get 'Radio Tokyo' on the radio? It is a propaganda program in which they play some swing pieces and give the Nip version of the news. A woman, 'Madam Tokyo', gives the news which is wildly fantastic and causes a lot of laughter and amusement. A few days ago when our planes got 89 planes at Wewak, M. Tokyo claims we lost 90 to their one. If half her claims were correct we'd have quit long ago instead of just starting to fight.

"Today someone put a sign on a bulletin board saying, 'If you consider work a pleasure you can certainly have a lot of fun in this Squadron'. The men haven't lost their sense of humor even though everyone feels pretty low at times—now and then we can pick up a little news on a radio we got out of an old airplane, but it isn't very clear as a rule. Of course, we have first hand news of this locality. Unfortunately, I can never write about it until after it has appeared in the news."

* * * *

February 12, 1944: "Yesterday Joe Christopher and four doctor friends dropped in on me. They were all navy doctors attached to the Marines. It was sure swell to see Joe again. We talked over old times we had together. I took them around to see our shops and some planes. They stayed for dinner and in the afternoon I took them out to the battle field. Then we went for a bath in the river. They all thought you and Lois Marie very all right when I showed them your pictures.

"Today I drew up plans for an incinerator. We are attempting to keep sanitary conditions as high as possible. They are necessary for good health. The plans I drew for our latrines have been copied by Headquarters and sent to every outfit over here.

"There's been a lot of activity the last few days. We have some pilots staying here, and we've been able to get first hand accounts of all missions. The Nips have been only on the defensive for some time now. They can't seem to scrape enough together for offensive operations. A lot of activity means a lot of work, but it is good to see activity. It makes one feel like something is being done."

"About the man whose wife had a baby after he'd not seen her for14 months. A bit too late, I think. Well, I've had a couple of men come to me with similar problems. I'll be darned if I know, why me. Do I look like Dorothy Dix or the Voice of Experience or something? Well, anyway I tried not to look too surprised and listened to their troubles. You probably know what I told them. Cancel their allotments, quit writing, and apply for divorce. Maybe I'm cruel, but such things I don't approve of."

* * * *

February 20, 1944: "Lois Marie is learning so fast. Now she is sitting up, learning to play with toys, and eating a variety of foods from a spoon. I guess she won't be eating any steaks for awhile though. How is rationing affecting you now? Are conditions worse than they were at Waycross? If not, they aren't so bad because we sure had good eats there. Today I took a couple of hours off and went to a native village. We got a couple of good pictures, but they weren't so good. The natives are getting lazy and don't want to pose unless they are paid for it. 'Picture two bobs' is their answer. That's the first time I've had off since the dance on Jan. 2nd. I don't mind working because there's no place to go anyway.

"Two sweet letters and a sweet valentine make me in high spirits tonight. If mail continues to come in as it has in the last few days I shall soon be caught up on your letters. I haven't received any snapshots yet, but am patiently waiting.

"Got a letter from my old college room mate today. Arnie is still working for Pan American Airways. At one of his stations in the Pacific he met an English girl and they were married. They are now separated too, but in June he expects to be able to take her to the States. Maybe someday we'll meet, the four of us. I'm going to write to him tonight and tell him all about Lois Marie."

* * * *

February 23, 1944: "Thank you, darling, for the snapshots which came in your letter today. Even at the early age of eleven days our Lois was a lovely baby. I am so happy about our baby.

"I often think of Dad's offer to go into business with him. It has many good features. The only one that I don't like so well is leaving Engineering. My final decision and yours will have to wait until I get home."

* * * *

February 25, 1944: "Today is your birthday. I hope that it is a happy one. I'm sorry I'm not there to help you celebrate. I think that next year I will. I hope you have received my little gift by now.

"I'm sorry that last night did not allow time for my usual daily letter. I had a program of soldier talent to put on. We pulled a couple of trailers together for a stage and strung up some lights. We had a GI band and some local talent. We had a huge crowd, and it went over big. I didn't get done until quite late and was very, very tired.

"I received a Christmas card from Sarah and O.B. today. Over here Christmas greetings are strung out over months. It is a reminder of a day that didn't mean much to us last year, but a hope for a real Christmas this next Dec.

"I received a bulletin from L.S.A. *(Lutheran Student Association)* yesterday. It was interesting reading. We shall always have a warm spot for L.S.A. because it was there that we met and had an opportunity to get to know each other just a little. That 'little' was the spark that lit the flame in our hearts. Just the other day, I wrote of a honeymoon when I get back, and today you suggest the same thing.

Yes, darling, it is definitely decided then. Our thoughts are always running parallel. Often our letters pass on the way to each other with identical thoughts and expressions. I like to think it is because of our love for each other.

"My, my … So Lois Marie already has three admirers. I never thought it would start this soon. She is definitely not a wall flower. Actually she must have a lot of admirers from the praise she gets from everyone who writes to me. How I'd like to see the little darling. I have the three snapshots you sent before me. What beautiful girls I have. How could a man be anything but a family man with two prizes like you.…

"I am enclosing a copy of a pamphlet that our planes drop upon the Japs. It tells them they are beaten and better quit. I found it rather interesting. Notice that everything is in reverse order. To start reading one would start at what we would call page 4, in the lower right hand corner and read vertically toward the top of the page and then go to the bottom and start on the 2nd row, etc. They are simplified for the poorly educated people and the more elaborate characters for the higher class. You can easily spot the difference.

"Yesterday our troops made a landing on the Admiralty Islands. They are in a strategic location to blockage the Japanese bases of Rabaul and Wewak. It is another big step in our progress. The last couple of months have seen a lot of history being made. There is still so much to be done though.

"Today I stopped in to see a couple of Aussie friends. We talked over the war situation and about home, of course. One gave me several lemons so I made some lemonade to drink at supper time. There are a few lemons growing in the wild country. They are small and very sour, but good. We have been getting a little fresh food lately and it sure is welcome."

* * * *

March 2, 1944: "There are so many bugs flying around that I can hardly write for swatting them. They seem to be holding a convention in our tent every night. I suppose spring work has started to show itself in Minnesota. I always liked spring better than any other season. The spring we spent at the University was the most memorable one. It was then that we got to know one another. The newsreels, the talks on the Knoll, the walks we had together made us realize more and more that we were meant to be Mr. and Mrs. Then the following spring with meetings every weekend at our homes or on the campus. Those were happy days. Your patience with me during those terrible moods was wonderful. I don't know why I was that way except the uncertainty of everything."

* * * *

March 3, 1944: "I am getting along fine, darling. I'm still feeling ok. I haven't had a sick day yet. My mind can be pretty much at ease knowing you and little Lois are in such good hands. I shall always be grateful to our folks for keeping you through the months of pregnancy and now with the baby to keep all your time occupied. When our day finally comes I will be thrilled to take over my rightful responsibility as father and husband.

"I'm enclosing another *Guinea Gold*. It will make good material to remember New Guinea by. I think it is a swell little paper. It gives one a maximum of news in a minimum of words. I hope you find them interesting.

"Our days go on about the same as usual with our duties to perform and sidelights such as news, rumors, ball games, fresh food to make things more interesting. Mail call is and always will be the most popular time of the day.

"Last night I gave a Chemical Warfare demonstration on first aid, protective measures and contamination. You see we are prepared for any eventuality. If the Japs use gas we will be ready to protect ourselves and counter with an offensive 100 times greater.

"The men feel kinda bad tonight. This is the fifth straight day with no mail at all. We know they are on the way, but our patience is short. I just returned from a ball game. Tonight we played an outfit that had beat us twice before. It was kind of a grudge game. They came over with about $200.00 waiting to be bet on their team. Some of our men called the bet. With two outs in the last inning one of our boys got a double and the following man drove him home beating them 1 to 0. It was an exciting game.

"Today is dreary and raining. Rain has such a depressing influence here. It makes one feel even more lonely than usual. Together we always enjoyed rain for its freshness and cleanliness. We shall again. I got hold of a Dec. 27th issue of LIFE today. It had some pictures and descriptions of this theater that are very accurate. I enjoyed them very much.

"All day I've been hoping for a letter and tonight two came. They make me feel very good because they were like you talking to me. Every letter is wonderful. The people back home are giving us wonderful support in their purchase of bonds, saving of salvageable materials, and their morale building. The people of Providence must be really on the ball with their record on the 4th drive. Yes, the Jap atrocities are terrible. I could tell you of many more that have never been released because of censorship.

"Lois must be getting to be quite a big girl to be eating out of a spoon and drinking out of a glass. You made me smile when you said she was a 'chip off the old block'; which chip? I can remember a day when I was about 3 or 4 and supposed to be asleep in the next room when I heard my Aunt Esther tell Mother that about me.

"My, you have versatile hair. I don't believe I ever saw the 'page boy' style on you. You haven't changed a bit in that respect. Changing your hair style is a bit of your creative instincts. I never knew when I'd come home to a new one. Your hair is one of your most beautiful assets. It is soft, blonde, and shining in any style, but I do have a couple of favorites.

"I'm smoking an old stinky cigar that I got from an Aussie. If I had this 'rope' at home you'd probably chase me out of the house with it. Cigars are awfully smelly things, I'll admit.

"By the way, I saw where some guy named Sinatra or something was called the most popular singer last year. I heard him the other day and he sounded only average to me. I hear that a lot of women are going nuts over him. How come he's so popular?

"I hope you soon receive my woolens. They'll probably be moldy. I wish I'd known where we were going so I could have left them. There is quite a bit of money tied up in them.

"Darling, the only thing that I'd like sent is some film. PD 16Agfa or its equivalent. We are pretty well supplied with toilet articles and cigarettes for some time. I'll enclose a note to the postmaster requesting authority to send film, if you can get any. I know film is extremely hard to get. Thanks for the jokes. I enjoy them. Mom sends me jokes, too. They do help cheer a person up.

"We're up to our neck in work tonight. There are seven men in this tent so it is hard to do much concentration. We'll probably be working most of the night. Work is like our mail. It comes in spurts.

"I was surprised by the number of steers and pigs that your Dad's got. I knew he and Gordon were very busy, but I never knew they had undertaken so much. They are really doing their part to win this war, aren't they? We can be proud that our families are doing their part.

"This may reach you late, but I hope you got a pen for Dad's birthday. They must be hard to find, but if you can find a good one I'm sure he'd appreciate it. I never saw him with a good pen in my life.

"Yesterday morning I caught a plane for (can't tell). I had to see a couple of colonels on some Squadron business. I didn't finish last night so borrowed a canvas cot and a blanket and stayed overnight. It was rather a damp night, and I didn't sleep much. Tonight I'm going to bed early. I finished my business this morning and finally after a few hours caught a 'hop' back here. I got to see some new scenery from the air. I'm always impressed with the beauty of this country from the air. It's too bad it isn't as nice here on the ground."

* * * *

March 15, 1944: "Captain Bundschuh is now Major Bundschuh. His recommendation has been in for a long time and surprised him by coming through. I'll be glad when I'll be eligible for Captain. Major B. said he'd recommend me the day I become eligible, i.e. enough overseas service. Today I got the February *Reader's Digest.* It came through very fast as a result of your letter. I'm going to read just part of it tonight.

"I'm so glad you are taking movies to keep a record of Lois Marie. It will be a great help for me in catching up on some of the things I'm missing. There is no 8 mm film projector here so I'm afraid I'll have to wait to see them.

"Here it is a hot Sunday evening. It has been scorching hot for a couple of days. In the tent the heat is terrific. The only bearable place at all is in the shade somewhere, but we can't work in the shade much so we just have to sweat it out. I went to the river tonight for a bath. The water was very refreshing, but when I got back here I was wringing wet again. We've all got used to wearing damp clothes. If I didn't drink so much water I'd be better off, but you know me and how I like water.

"Soon it will be time to go to church. I missed last week so I'll go tonight. I miss the friendly smiles and greetings in a church at home. People have a way of making you feel at home. Then I like the reverent atmosphere of a real church with the singing, the organ, and its quietness. It's the best place in the world to think.

"Some of the men have started a new hobby. They found there are a lot of rare species of butterflies over here and have started collecting them. I haven't started. I don't think Lt. Young would make a good impression on the men if I were to start tripping around in a pair of shorts with a net, a determined look in my eyes, a trail of dust and two mental doctors behind me. Would you like to have me start? Then in my spare time I could run over hill and dale and through people's back yards and gardens in eager pursuit of the species Lepidoptra when I return. You could cheer me on.

"You mention Lois Marie bubbling and suggested she may be getting teeth. Isn't it awfully early for our baby to start getting teeth? I know she's a remarkable little girl, but I thought babies didn't start to get teeth until 11 to 13 months old. Maybe I'm wrong. *(Lois got her first tooth at 5 months and one week.)*

"I'm glad you found Dad's serious side. I imagine a lot of people think he is all humor, but he's really underneath it all quite a thinker. I often sat down with him like you must have done and talked with him about all kinds of subjects."

* * * *

March 23, 1944: "Again it is raining and I'm going through the procedure of dodging drops and insects. It's not pleasant at all when it rains here. Even though it does cool off considerably it is still dreary. The bugs are always bad. When I get back to the States they shouldn't bother me much after becoming accustomed to them here.

"I'm feeling fine as usual and getting along pretty good. I've had a little trouble with fungus in my ears, but Doc's got it pretty well licked. Everything molds over here, even inside the ears. A lot of men have skin trouble too. The skin just rots off and new comes on. We call it the 'Guinea Rot'.

"Today the news was released of the invasion of two more islands just above Kavieng, New Ireland. I think we've got the Nips worried. They don't know where we'll strike next. We have practically cut off all their supplies to many of their bases. I haven't seen a Jap plane in a long time. The Russians' tremendous driving power and the continuous bombing of Germany are good news from that theater.

"A new personnel rotation plan is being put into effect in this theater. After 18 months overseas a man is eligible to return to the States. His priority is determined by a point system. For every month in a rear area we get 1 pt. and for each month in a combat zone we get 3 pts. We have about 6 months in a forward area so our priority shouldn't be too low. The big trouble is that there is a lack of shipping space now and they aren't keeping up with the eligibles at all. We can hope that when our time is on the list we'll be caught up, or better yet that the war will be over.

"A letter from Mom today written after you'd left was a little sad and lonely. They love you like a daughter and Lois Marie too. She said the house was too quiet and dull, and went on to explain about the talking and sewing you'd done. Darling, in your sweet way you've won the hearts of not only me but a family. We have four generations involved in love and friendship; from our grandparents to little Lois Marie. We can be proud of this accomplishment.

"Three pictures of Lois Marie came today. Thank you very much, darling. Isn't she a lovely little darling? All three pictures are very good, and I've already shown them to a lot of men. I gotta do a little bragging once in a while. I'm glad you like the coin bracelet. Yes, I made it. You can see that I'm not such a hot metal worker. I'm sorry it didn't arrive for your birthday.

"Did I tell you about the home brew, or 'jungle juice' as we call it, that is made here? Those that think they must have their liquor have used their American ingenuity to do evil. They concoct their potion by two methods: by drilling a hole to insert sugar into a coconut, then sealing and aging it until the desired 'kick' is obtained. A few of the Kentucky boys with civilian experience have, in spite of the 'revenooing' efforts of the officers, set up highly successful stills as a refinement of the first method. The result is a purple liquid with the delightful (?) tang of a 50-50 solution of kick-a-poo juice and carbolic acid. Well, now they have it and before it eats up the container they have to decide whether they should use it for some worthy purpose such as paint remover or let it scar their stomach tissues in its intended utility of making brutes of men. I am sorry to say the latter is usually chosen. Needless to say me, without an impervious gut and a certain sense of morals, have retained my position 'on the wagon'.

"Four of your letters came today with four more pictures of Lois Marie, all very cute and sweet. I'm so anxious to hold her and talk to her.

"It is just 6:30, but it is already dark. This near the equator there is little difference in the length of days throughout the year. It is almost always twelve hours of dark and equally of light. Recently Australia set its clocks back an hour and we followed suit.

"I received a copy of the Lutheran Alumni Fellowship today. Did you give them my address? L.S.A. seems essentially the same. Through it we came to know each other. From L.S.A. I first took you home to meet Esther and to spend a couple of hours with you showing me a book on art and taking a beating in Chinese Checkers. That was the first time we were alone together to start the process of getting to know each other. The process didn't take long. We spent very few hours together before we knew we were in love. I think that memorable day at Taylor's Falls we must have been very sure. All these memories are like a dream."

* * * *

April 4, 1944: "4/4/44: Look at that date. That occurs only every 11 years 1 month and 1 day. I wonder if on May 5, 1955 I'll notice that date too. I often notice such things. I guess that I've worked so much with numbers that I give them special attention.

"Rumors have become popular. Few if any of them have any foundation, but there are always two or three of them floating around. A common greeting is, 'Have you heard any new rumors?' And one seldom gets a negative answer. Some people start them just to see how long it takes to get back to them. A typical one might be, 'This outfit is going to be shipped to Miami Beach to train WACs'. Another popular pastime is gambling. Poker and dice are the most popular. One can always see a couple of games going. The games aren't always small either. One man made $1700.00 coming across on the boat. It is common to see three or four hundred dollars tied up in a game. The reason is probably because of the lost sense of the value of money over here. The average man thinks of the Australian pound as being equal to the American dollar while actually it is worth three and one-half times as much. There are few places to spend money so any man with something to sell can usually find a buyer. I saw a portable radio worth about ten dollars sold to a colored Lt. for seventy pounds or about $224.00. Men pay fifteen pounds ($48) for a bottle of whiskey. Men on Guadalcanal used their silver dollars to see how far they could sail them. These are exceptions.

"You might wonder what happens to the money I receive. Officers have to pay twenty-five cents a meal, and lately I've had to buy almost all new clothes and shoes. My watch took more than one month's pay of $20.00. So I manage to stay broke. You, darling, are doing the saving there. I'm so proud of how you've been managing our finances. We will have good use for the money and will have a good time buying the things we need.

"Doc is mounting two plates of butterflies. He had a good background in zoology, so he finds them more interesting that the average man.

"It has been raining. Our tents are getting old and leak pretty bad, and those who have outside work can't stop just for a rain. The area is a sea of mud and puddles. Tomorrow all the puddles will have to be sprayed with oil as a part of our malaria control program. Oil prevents the anopheles mosquito from breeding."

* * * *

April 9, 1944: "Easter Sunday. Our Easter parade was unique. As the men filed into their trucks to go to work I noticed a few of the better outfits. The first man wore a dainty pair of shorts cut from an old pair of pants. It was unique in that one leg was about four inches longer than the other. They were held safely in place with a stout piece of rope. His hat was a new creation called the 'Guinea Droop'. Another wore a two-piece suit with a unique color scheme. The slacks had been colored by a special process of sliding into third base, into a rich black. The shirt blended nicely being a brown pastel. The hat, a collegiate model (none) was the best for the day. The visor type of cap with either the uplift bill or the soggy sag has become increasingly popular since being introduced by Adrian. The latest in shirt style calls for no buttons and a loose hanging shirttail which also has the practical use as a napkin or grease rag. The trend in footwear is the new unpolished boot type ranging from destroyers to 12EE. Neckties, gardenias, pleats, puffed sleeves and matching accessories are conspicuous by their absence. Nevertheless, everyone was strictly 'in the mode'."

* * * *

April 10, 1944: "I'm glad you received the box of clothes, and I'm glad everything was in good condition. Yes, there are a lot of stories in that box. I'll tell you all about them when I return.

"A letter from Mom today held quite a surprise. She said they were going to buy the house next to Fausses. I think it is a grand idea (if Dad doesn't plunge too deeply in debt to buy it). For years they have dreamed of a new house. This house isn't new but it is very nice and comfortable. Living next to Fausses will be a nice feature too.

"Many thanks for the 100 cigarettes that came in the mail today. They were in very good condition. I've got quite a good stock of cigarettes now. We get issues quite regularly, but the extra ones come in handy. These are fresh so I'll save them and use the others first. The Aussies go for our cigarettes in a big way. Their brands are more expensive, harder to get, and very inferior. I get quite a lot of enjoyment out of smoking. Over here anything distracting from general duties is recreation. I think that when I get back if you wish I will stop smoking. There is one thing that I do need. I have only one package of razor blades left. I was well-stocked when I left, but I've used them all now. Would you please send me as many packages as you can get, single edge blades."

* * * *

April 11, 1944: *100th Service Squadron, A.P.O. 322, c/o Postmaster San Francisco, California.* "Somewhere in New Guinea. For the three previous nights I haven't been able to write. My reason: I have been busy in the most liberal sense of the word. In the last three days I've had only two meals, a couple hours sleep under the wing of an airplane, and no bath until an hour ago. Now everything is just swell. I've finished a big meal, swam in the ocean, and have a canvas cot to sleep on as soon as it gets dark." *(Lyle's move brought him to Finschhafen.)*

"I had a plane ride this morning, really enjoyed the cool air above the clouds. That's the only place a man can cool off over here. There'll be no more floors in tents, showers, mess hall, and such luxuries for us for a long time now. It was nice while it lasted."

* * * *

April 18, 1944: "I got my good night's sleep last night and felt very good today in spite of rain and mud. It rained most of the night and a good part of the day. Consequently, our area is mud inches deep everywhere inside and outside. Now without a floor it is hard to keep anything dry. Even in the mess hall there are about three inches of mud. You can imagine the job the cooks have trying to work sanitarily. In spite of mud and everything morale is very good. The men are anxious for activity and will probably really 'go to town' when we start operations again.

"We got some new men yesterday, and one was from Canby. He used to drive for the Canby Shipping Association, and said he often stopped at Dad's filling station and knew Dad very well. He said 'the man' always used to kid him a lot so there is no mistake it was Dad.

"This afternoon I had a long jeep trip to take. The roads were slippery and rough. Normally they are hard to drive with steep hills and sharp turns. I had chains on all four wheels and much of the way had to use four wheel drive in the lowest position. Only a jeep and an army truck could get through such roads."

* * * *

April 19, 1944: "This is a bit nicer place than the last. There are a lot of palm trees and high hills. The ocean is near and the beaches are full of coral. The coral is very pretty, but rough on the feet. I was swimming for a short time yesterday, but the salt water made me feel awfully sticky, and we don't have a shower to use afterwards. The sore spot of this area is the gooey, sticky mud. The roads are awfully slippery. Last night my jeep skidded into a truck with no lights on. The truck was parked in my lane and when I saw it I swerved around him, but the back of the jeep didn't follow the front and it nicked the truck. The damage is already repaired."

* * * *

April 19, 1944: *(a V-mail).* "I'm sitting in the orderly room with my raincoat on holding down a chair and a ration box with my feet. People in the States might think this a little rough, but they don't realize the facts. There are many that don't enjoy the convenience of running water. We, lucky group, have running water in, or should I say, through our tents. It is not a stinky little trickle like comes out of a faucet, but a stinky big flow four inches deep. It is enough to automatically remove all scraps of paper and rearrange the furniture. There goes somebody's shoe through. Oh well, it probably didn't fit him too good anyway. I have been debating whether in this leaky tent it is raining harder inside or outside. The tent is doing a good job of straining the water. We have always wanted to live near a lake and now I'm in one. I'm going to try to rent a boat and go back to my tent. I hope my canvas (bathtub) cot is still there. What a wonderful night, Your wet, Lyle."

* * * *

April 20, 1944: "Last night I wrote you a crazy V-mail letter after the other letter. I was just sitting with nothing to do and wrote the first thing that came to my head. It may sound awfully silly, so maybe it is best to ignore that letter.

"I got myself an automatic rifle. I don't care for the 45 pistol I had so I got something more accurate. I'd like to keep it for hunting after the war."

April 25, 1944. There is a lot to be done. This afternoon I took a bunch of men down to pick up rations for the outfit for a few days. We all got soaked, but nobody minded. If you don't hear from me for a few days, don't worry. I'll be very, very busy.

* * * *

April 28, 1944: "It has been three days since I've written you. The reason isn't because I haven't wanted to, but because I haven't found it possible. I am writing this on a real table, sitting on a real chair in a stateroom. It is a little difficult to write because of the rocking and rolling. On this boat I've enjoyed some luxuries I haven't seen for eight months. A hot water shave, ice in the tea, and a bunk with a mattress. We're all very swell. Unfortunately just the officers get this sort of treatment. I feel almost guilty enjoying such things while the men still eat and sleep in the old way. The cool ocean breezes are sure refreshing. After three days without sleep and without a real meal I can't seem to get too much sleep or food." *(Lyle was on the way to Aitape.)*

* * * *

Lyle spent just eleven days at Finschhafen, from April 17 to April 28th, 1944: Then his Squadron moved by ship to Aitape, and by April 30th was there.

* * * *

April 28, 1944: "For three days we went through hell. There was hard, back-breaking work to be done in a certain time. There was no time for sleep and no facilities for eating. Occasionally the men would get hold of a can of stew and gulp it down, but there were no meals. Throughout the time there was much rain and the mud was deep and sticky. Everyone had wet shoes filled with mud. Trucks going by would splatter it all over everyone. When things would slow down a little the men would go down to the beach and wade in, clothes, shoes and all to get some of the mud off and come out somewhat refreshed to go to work again. It was rough, but now it's over and the work has been accomplished. I know now what FDR meant when he said, 'War is Hell'.

"The war news continues to look very good. The recent invasion of Hollandia and other points in New Guinea is a big step in cleaning up this locality. I wish this boat was headed to the Golden Gate instead of (secret)." *(Aitape.)*

* * * *

May 3, 1944: "We are pretty well set up again. Our area is in a palm grove. After clearing out the brush and old coconuts it is quite nice. The men have built a mess shelter out of logs and all other necessary construction such as latrines, garbage pits, water tanks, and tents are all set up. I'm in a tent with Doc Stouse and Schilling. We three get along better than any other combination, so we'll probably be tent mates from now on. Schilling is a Captain now. He made it just a few days ago after about a year and a half as a 1st Lt.

"There is a beautiful beach near here for swimming, a lot like the beach at Venice. We are far beyond the luxuries of shows, etc., now so go to bed about 8 p.m. and rise early for work. There is little to do for recreation except talk about the news and everyday happenings here."

* * * *

May 4, 1944: "It's been a wonderful day. Everything is right with the world again. Yes, I got six letters from you. I've been laughing and joking all day. I enjoyed the bully beef for supper and found myself whistling or humming several times. The change in the men after the mail comes is nothing short of miraculous.

I got over my ear trouble. The fungus growth is a form of mold formed by bacterial action rather than a parasite. The medical branch of the army is doing a splendid job to counter all the odd ills that a man picks up over here.

"I've seen quite a few Jap prisoners. Most of them are small and run-down looking, but some are big brutes and well-fed. I've had the opportunity to examine a lot of their equipment. Caution must be used because of booby traps, but they're cleaned out now.

"The news today is of the rescue of 100 missionaries that had been held by the Japs. They had been forced to follow the army and build roads, etc. The women were badly treated, brutally ... when this is over the resulting peace must be formed so that it is a lasting one."

* * * *

May 12, 1944: "The two coins are Japanese. I don't know their value. Rather than using silver, they use aluminum. The paper bill is not real Japanese money (notice the English writing.) This is invasion money. The Japs were so confident of taking Australia that they printed their own money so as to make their plundering appear to be buying. It seems they wasted a lot of paper and ink."

* * * *

May 18, 1944: "It is windy up here on the bridge. The sun is shining, but there is a good breeze blowing to keep one cool. The ship isn't as nice as some I've been on, but it is still ok. The chow is good and the work light. Sleeping is a problem. Down in the hold of the ship is terribly hot and stuffy. We sleep three high and about 24 to a room the size of your kitchen. With our gear spread all over the place, there's not much room to move around … I have seen a lot of interesting sights the last few days. You will get some idea if you read the paper for this date."

Air bases were needed on the island of Wakde, but the Japanese were in the way. Lyle recalled that big guns on the island had pounded Wakde and six waves of boats carrying our troops headed in. It took two more days of fighting to clear the island, but even before the shooting stopped engineers and aviation technicians went to work rebuilding and enlarging the airfield. In a matter of days, the airfield was ready to use.

Lyle recalled that as his Squadron disembarked the LST at Wakde, the Japanese ineffectively shot at them in a nuisance ploy. There was no time to set up tents before dark, so men had to sleep wherever they could find a spot. Lyle slept in the cab of a truck. During the night about 25 remaining Japs began a banzai (suicide) attack between the engineering outfit and the 100th Service Squadron. All the Japs were killed, no Allied losses.

The next evening after trying to set up tents, all the men were hot and sweaty. No water supply. Bulldozers dug a pit below sea level until water seeped in to fill it. In the meantime the men drilled many holes in lengths of pipe that they strung between trees. They pumped water into a big tank, which flowed through the pipe making an innovative shower. Two hundred naked men walked through the sprinkling water, got wet; the water was turned off while they soaped up. Then the water was turned on, and the men walked through again to get rinsed off. It was the only way so many men could take a shower with a limited amount of water.

* * * *

May 23, 1944: "We've had a rough time for a week now. Everyone is all worked out. Sleeping is the biggest problem. It's not easy sleeping in a foxhole. The sand keeps running down your neck and the rats, lizards, land crabs, and insects are poor company. I spent four nights in one of those foxholes. If it were not for censorship, I could almost write a book about our experiences in the past ten days. It has been an experience I wouldn't have missed for a lot, but one I don't want to go through again.

"Today, I've been supervising the building of latrines and mess hall, etc...."

* * * *

May 29, 1944: "In addition to my other duties, I'm also Acting Commander Officer while Maj. Bundshuh is gone for awhile ... The heat and flies on this island are some of our worst problems. It is almost impossible to control flies without screen-in mess halls, latrines, and other buildings; to do so requires men and materials, which are difficult to spare ... Army life is just a process of confronting problems and solving them. This is a twenty-four hour job ... war is a day and night affair."

"I have some men making a mobile unit. We are outfitting the back of a truck with bins, drawers, and shelves for nuts, bolts, screws, and small parts. When this truck is finished, I'm going to have another set up with special tools. By doing this, we'll have everything in better order, easier found, and thus more efficient ... there's been lots of flying activity lately, which gives all of our departments all the work they can handle. I t sometimes requires the switching of men to handle a phase of work that has become a problem. We're keeping 'em flying."

* * * *

June 6, 1944: "I got out of the hospital this morning. I'm still a little weak but otherwise ok. I'll just have to take it easy for a couple of days." *Lyle had dengue fever. As this book was written he recalled that during his stay at the hospital (a series of tents) there was an attack by the Japanese. When the soldiers heard the warning of three artillery shells being shot off, they had seconds to make their way to the trenches to find cover. Those who were mobile had to get there on their own, so the ones on stretches could be carried to safety. When the attack was over they discovered that the hospital had been destroyed. Those who could walk away were told to go back to their unit. A rather violent way of being 'discharged'.*

* * * *

June 8, 1944: "Well, the invasion of Europe has finally started. Hope it goes well with as little bloodshed as possible. By the end of the month we should have a good idea of how it is going to turn out.

"I've lost quite a bit of weight lately, about 20 pounds, for which I'm glad. I will probably gain it all back when life eases up a bit." *A few days later Lyle wrote,* "I'm feeling stronger after my illness. I've a pretty good appetite again and will soon be my old self again. We've been exceptionally busy lately so I'll be glad when I can give my all again."

* * * *

June 12, 1944: "Today I've been in the army two years. It seems like an awfully long time. Remember that day a couple years ago then you, the family, and I went to Monte to catch the draftee bus. None of us felt very good that day. There was an uncertainty about the future that bothered me a lot. We didn't know then that marriage and a few months together were possible before the war was over. As it has turned out things are pretty good in comparison. The few months together were wonderfully happy."

Wakde Island: 1944

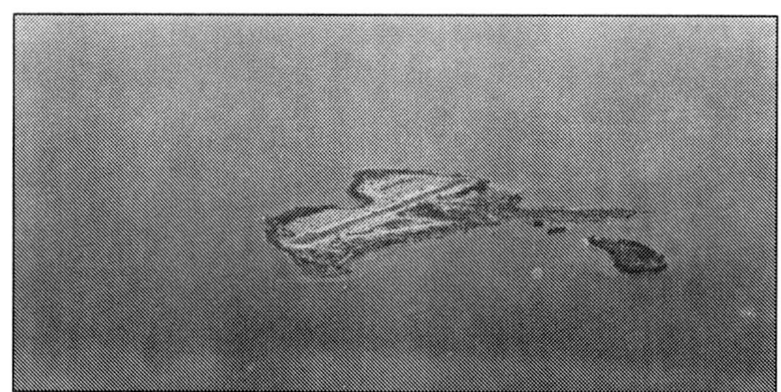

Island of Wakde, off the coast of New Guinea

Lyle with his Jeep named Lois

Squadron area and tents

Officer's Shacks. Lyle lived in the furthest one.

Squadron Mess Hall

Their dear, dear foxhole. It saved them many times during bombing raids.

Crews at work. Note the bombed out palm trees.

Crews at work on damaged airplane

A bomb once blew the near-half off the mess hall.
Note the clothes on a line after washing them in an oil barrel of warm water.

April 30, 1944. Beautiful palm trees on Aitape, New Guinea

Aussie friends. The Aussies completed very dangerous missions in New Guinea.

Men of the 336th

The 336th Service Squadron, New Guinea

Morotai, Dutch East Indies: 1944

Bob Hope (left) and Frances Langford (center) entertain the troops on Morotai

Soldiers watching the USO show, September 1944

Jerry Colombo and Bob Hope perform

On board ship heading to the Philippines
Captain Lyle Young, Lt. Herman, and Lt. Bowerman

June 14, 1944: "Yesterday was THE red letter day of my whole overseas service. I got 18, yes 18 letters from you, 4 from home, and one from Betty Ann *(my sister.)* It took me a couple hours to read them all, two of the happiest hours I've had over here. The letters were dated all through May from the 1st to the 23rd. Darling, at the rate our bank account is growing we will have two or three thousand dollars to begin our life together. Keep up the good work, honey. I haven't been paid in three months now and don't care if I wait three months more. I have no need for money now, anyway. There's absolutely no place to spend it anywhere around here."

* * * *

June 16, 1944: "Yesterday's mail brought a letter and a package from you with two rolls of film and some caramels which were melted but tasted good. Thank you, sweety. I shall try to get a picture for you. I don't know where I'll have it developed. We can't send undeveloped film so I won't promise any date on the picture, but it will come eventually.

"Today is hot and dusty. As the planes take off they kick up a lot of dust which blows over into our shops in big clouds. It is quite a problem at times because some of our shops can't work when the air is dusty, i.e. parachutes can't be packed, etc. The raid of our planes on Japan has caused a lot of talk and speculation. The B-29s that did the job are wonderful planes. The war in this theater is full of surprises."

* * * *

June 19, 1944: "I just finished a tour around to the planes we are fixing. They are all coming along pretty good. I've promised the men a half day off a week to wash clothes when we get caught up a little, and it looks like they're working for that. No one has had a day off for a couple months now. Things like dirty clothes really pile up quickly. The men in the army have learned to appreciate laundry service. There are a lot of things that we used to take for granted that are realistic now.

"An order from higher headquarters has got us working long hours now. We get up at 4:30, start work at 6 and quit work at 6:30 p.m. Quite often (like last night) there are certain things to tend to that take up the evening so on those days there are no daylight hours off. It is a little tough but will only be for a couple of weeks so (I hope). As long as our efforts will help to hasten the end of the war no one is going to gripe very much.

"Glad to hear O.B. and Sarah are 'expecting'. I think they took their cue from us. Hearing how happy we are over our little daughter must have made them change their minds about waiting. I'm sure happy we have Lois Marie. Life would be less interesting without her. Thanks for the Father's Day card. I can tell you it is quite a thrill to be honored on a man's first Father's Day."

"If ever there was a scorching day, this is it. If these are the South Sea Islands they talk about and show in pictures somebody sure got a misconception. Anyway this is some better than New Guinea. Of course, that doesn't take much."

* * * *

June 25, 1944: "It was a year ago tonight when you left on the train from Waycross. That was the saddest day of my life. Today we have a year less of being apart to wait out. I hope we never have to endure another length of time like that apart. It has been a terribly long year. Without the thought of the future's happiness it would have been unbearable. I need you so very much."

* * * *

June 25, 1944: *336th Service Squadron, A.P.O. 565-1, c/o Postmaster San Francisco, California* "Did you notice my change of address? I've been transferred to another outfit where I'll hold the same job. I'm not sure why I was transferred, but was told that I was needed here. I sure hated to leave the 100th. I had learned to know every man and now will have all that to do over."

* * * *

June 30, 1944: "A rather amusing thing happened today. Somebody asked what day of the week it was. Everyone gave out their guesses which covered practically them all. I guessed it was Tuesday. Well, the calendar proved it was Friday. I tell this to illustrate that every day here is the same. It will be swell when Sunday means a day of worship and rest again, as God intended it to be.

"I guess we'll be paid in Dutch money this month. Their basic amount is the guilder worth about 53 cents. Again we'll have to learn a new monetary system. I don't understand why we are to use Dutch money. There are no towns or Dutch anywhere near here now. The Dutch government is in exile in London, I guess. I'll send some coins."

* * * *

July 4, 1944: "Did I ever tell you about my desire to be active in Boy Scout work? Ever since I was old enough to belong I've wanted to get back in as a leader. Of course, I've lost my desire for camping out, but I should be able to overcome those difficulties.

"We've got a plane ready for a test hop this morning and I'm waiting for the pilot now. The crew that repaired the plane were in and wanted me to go along. They evidently have a lot of faith in their work. Well, I have too for that matter.

"Today I saw a big crowd of men gathered around a plane. I drove over to see what the excitement was. There was a nurse in a pair of coveralls with the plane. Everyone was standing there staring. Rather an odd situation, isn't it, but not so odd when you think that these men haven't seen a white woman in months. What a bunch of 'wolves' we'll be when we get back. You can be sure I'll confine my 'wolfing' to you, honey."

* * * *

July 7, 1944: "Sweetheart, keep sending your descriptions of all the antics and developments of the baby. I want to know when she gets a new tooth, says a new word, or learns a new trick. I try to visualize each of these things."

* * * *

July 8, 1944: "I spent all morning troubling over a faulty engine. Airplanes are as temperamental as artists. One minute they will operate perfectly and the next minute there will be something wrong with them. We treat them much as a doctor treats a patient. We list all the symptoms and think out possible sources of trouble. Each man is a specialist on one phase of the structure, such as electrician, instruments, engines, etc. After testing each system and making any necessary repairs we check again to make sure everything is ok."

* * * *

July 9, 1944: "If you were here this morning we could enjoy a walk along the beach. It is almost cool this morning and the ocean looks very blue. This is a beautiful place, but after the pre-invasion bombing and naval shelling its palm trees are in shambles. Then the army moved in with its bulldozers to carve roads and air field installations to further mar its natural beauty.

"Today baby is 8 months old. Those are eight months I've missed. I hope and pray that I won't miss many more of our baby's development. A Sgt. just saw me writing a letter and when I told him we write to each other almost every day he remarked, "You can't have been married very long.

"We have a pet in our hut now. We found a monkey that is very tame and quite amusing. Evidently the Japs brought him here. Right now he's got a rope all tangled up in a chair and is chattering for help. He's a funny little rascal. You should see him chew gum. Next door is a parrot which doesn't get along very well with the monkey. Quite a little zoo we have."

* * * *

July 19, 1944: "The Father's Day gift is wonderful. I've been carrying the picture with me all day and showing it to everyone. Lois is prettier than her previous pictures. The enclosed trinket is made from an Australian florin (.32). The set is a shell cut down. These shells are called cat's eyes by the men cuz they are white with a dark center like the pupil of any eye. The shell was originally round, but I filed it down and polished it.

"I saw a show last night, *Above Suspicion*, with Fred McMurray and Joan Crawford. Also got a package with the book *Life with Father*, a *Reader's Digest*, and the *Granite Tribune*. Thank you for the book, darling.

"I leave day after tomorrow for McKay, Australia, for a ten day rest leave. I'll fly down and back. I'm eagerly looking forward to the leave. I managed to borrow 30 pounds to finance the leave. Margie, did you send the check for $100? I'll need it to pay back my debt. McKay is a small town with not much to do, but I plan on getting a lot of sleep, eats, exercise, and shows."

* * * *

July 27, 1944: "Somewhere in Guinea. I've completed the first leg of my journey to Australia. I caught a plane yesterday morning and got here this afternoon. I am staying at a replacement camp, expect to be here a few days as transportation facilities aren't too good. I slept like a baby last night. Some of the officers in our group in Waycross are very near the camp here. I've enjoyed seeing them all. I've spent most of my time with Lt. Ray. We went to a show last night and spent the morning together. He is just out of the hospital and is awaiting reassignment to Australia. He has a leave coming and is hoping to go down with me. Today I ran into Blumenthal, the old 1st Sgt. in the 100th. Everyone remarked on all the weight I've lost and my 34 inch waist.

"Ray and I just took some pictures of each other with his camera. I moved into his tent this morning after his other tent mate left. We've been taking it very easy, just lying around talking, reading, and writing letters. What a way to fight a war, huh? My leave doesn't start until I get to McKay so this delay isn't cutting that short anyway."

* * * *

August 3, 1944: "Somewhere in Australia. I have reached my destination finally. I completed the last two laps of the journey yesterday. We spent almost the entire day flying. A good part of the day we were above the clouds and over water. From what I see so far I'll really enjoy my leave. Last night the Red Cross gave a barbeque, a whole steer roasted over hot coals for about 24 hours, and the meat was delicious. We also had some beer. The food here is swell. I had my first glass of milk in a year yesterday and a lot of other firsts in a long time.

"This is a nice clean little town, but there's not much to do. The American Red Cross runs the place where we billet and board and try to provide entertainment for the soldiers. They are doing a swell job. I'm staying at what once was an old home. I have a small room on a closed-in porch which is quite nice. There is a rumor that Eleanor Roosevelt slept here. Oh thrill."

* * * *

August 5, 1944: "By the way a reserve officer gets a bonus of $500 for every year of active service. That will add to our little nest egg too. I'm still having a good time. Night before last I spent at the Officer's Club talking with anyone who would listen and drinking some beer. I had my picture taken. The proofs will be ready Tuesday and they are to send the pictures to me at my A.P.O. Then I'll send one to you. Yesterday I bought a purse for you and a couple little ornaments for Betty Ann and our mothers, all of which I'm sending to you. I hope you like them. There is so little to buy, but I wanted to send some kind of souvenir from Australia."

* * * *

August 6, 1944: "I got up at 7 this morning and took another bicycle ride. It is fun to ride around and see the town. Almost everyone in town has a bicycle and there are very few cars. I've made a point to get acquainted with some Australians. They are a little more reserved than the average Yank. Their names for things are different from ours. For example: buns are scones, cookies are cakes, streetcars are trams, druggist is chemist, radios are wireless, and orange aide is orange squash.

"I just had breakfast. I had oatmeal, a small steak (yes, steak) and an egg with toast and milk. Now I'll have to take a bicycle ride to wear that off. The meals are sure swell. It will be hard to eat the chow when I get back up north. Yesterday I sat for a sketch which I'll send you. The old lady that made it just started sketching a few years ago. She did a good job on the eyes, and mouth, but I didn't like the chin, cheek and forehead line and the lack of chin which I have plenty of. So I made a lot of revisions. I also saw my proofs yesterday. I picked one in which I was wearing a leather jacket and cap." *(The picture is gorgeous.).*

* * * *

August 10, 1944: "They have a piano here and I tried to sit down and play the few tunes I used to know, but my fingers wouldn't do it. It wasn't much to forget, but I used to play a lot for my own enjoyment."

* * * *

August 12, 1944: "Yesterday three of us officers spent a pleasant afternoon in a little museum here in town. An old gentleman spent about three hours showing and explaining different things to us. We learned a lot about Australia, the great barrier reef, and the aborigines."

* * * *

August 14, 1944: "This is the last day of my leave. Tomorrow I start the long flight back to the outfit." *Lyle went on to tell of the shows he had seen, horseback riding, and other activities to make up the much needed rest and relaxation. Upon his return he had 29 letters from me. Some kind of record, and the check for $100 was included. Lyle reported,* "I feel the leave was a total success. It improved my health and fit me mentally for work again."

* * * *

August 18, 1944: "I have just been rereading your letters. They are wonderful morale builders, each is an inspiration and a tonic to me. It is so good to get back and get them all. Well, I'm in the old groove again. Everything is just about the same as usual. We have plenty to do in all departments. I spent all day just roaming around to see that was new and how the work was progressing. I am very pleased with the results the men have achieved while I was gone. Makes me proud of them.

"The recent pictures that came through were stuck together because the letter had been wet. I couldn't read the letter at all which was very disappointing, but by soaking the pictures I got them apart. I like them all. The ones of you and the grandparents with the baby are fine. I like the one where our little monkeyshine is wearing a hat. It is cute as anything.

"Tonight there is the show, *Birth of the Blues*, with Bing Crosby. That is one picture I'll not mind seeing again. Bing Crosby is always good in my estimation, although since Frankie came along I haven't been able to sleep nights.... sigh.

"Today Bob Hope, Frances Langford, and Jerry Colona were here and gave a good program. That's the first time any of the traveling shows have got up here to the front. It was a very good program for morale.

"Tomorrow I'm sending a box of odds and ends to you. There are several Yank magazines, a cigarette tray made from a mortar shell (needs painting), an Aussie pennant, a couple of things I've made from a salvaged parachute. One is a South Sea island skirt (not to be worn in public) and a woven belt in need of snaps. It will probably take a couple of months to reach you. None of its contents are very valuable, only things that might amuse you as souvenirs."

* * * *

August 26, 1944: "An outfit near here has everything FUBAR (Fouled up beyond all recognition), and they've been pestering us all morning. They want to borrow equipment, vehicles, tools and men. I guess I should have hung up a big NO sign on my desk and sent our men out to do their work, but I think we have the troubles all ironed out now. I hope so. Last night I was called out of our show three times by someone wanting this or that done. The show was *Million Dollar Baby* with Patricia Lane."

* * * *

August 27, 1944: "Today your letter of July 4th came. It must have been lost somewhere along the way. I'm going to have to write quite a few V-mail letters for awhile. The post office is out of airmail stamps and envelopes."

* * * *

August 29, 1944: "We've been very busy the last couple days again. We've run into some tough technical problems which we finally solved. It is this sort of thing that makes engineering work interesting.

"We've got the Nips guessing. They don't know where we'll strike next and I think they must be a little nervous. There is a lot of optimism among the men. They speculate a lot on when we'll go home. Guesses all the way from Christmas to the spring of 1946. The general consensus is that it will be next spring 1945: This we know for sure that I'll be home just as soon as I can get there legally.

"Today has been rainy. We don't mind the rain a great deal here because it isn't muddy. This island is almost entirely coral. Rain makes it cooler too which is a welcome relief from the cruel sun."

* * * *

September 2, 1944: "I look back on our wedding day. It was sure a busy afternoon, to buy the ring, meet the folks and then you, take a taxi to Urbana for the license and then a taxi to the church. I was afraid that my dad would play some crazy wedding march or something. But he realized the seriousness of the situation ok. It was a rapid ceremony but thrilling and unforgettable. The promises we make there will always be kept faithfully.

"Last night we had a full colonel stay with us. Never let it be said that we'll pass up a chance to do a little apple polishing. He was very pleasant and sociable and we enjoyed having him.

"Today Chico, the monkey, became a movie star. A couple of fellows borrowed him to be the narrator (?) of a film on the history of the island. I'd like to bring the monk home after the war, but we're not allowed to do that. He'll have to return to the wilds again.

"So you are suffering along with some dental work. It's best to keep up with it. My teeth seem to be holding up remarkably well considering the lack of calcium in our diets. It has been two years since I've had any work done, and I still have no apparent cavities.

"Life here is such a routine. The food is a little better with fresh meat occasionally. Our movie projector is broken so no more shows, but plenty of work if that can be called news.

"Today we had to dip our blankets in some kind of dip. It looked like water with soap and lime in it. They sure stink now. This dip is a precaution against typhus which is carried by a small mite. It is all disagreeable but worthwhile if it keeps sickness away.

"The weather continues to be hot, about 125 degrees in the shade. This is winter so the summers must really be rough. I don't mind the heat so much any more. I will really suffer when I have to go to a cold climate again.

"The show last night was with Hopalong Cassidy. The sound was so bad that I went back to my hut and read an old magazine. One of my room mates, Lt. Mason, gets the Colliers, so we have that to read from cover to cover.

"I have a book by Robert Benchley that I'm reading now. I always enjoyed his kind of humor. The title is *Inside Benchley*, a collection of short essays.

We had fresh eggs for breakfast this morning, the first time in two months. Have you ever tasted dehydrated eggs? They aren't good at all. That goes for anything dehydrated."

* * * *

September 17, 1944: *336 Service Squadron, A.P.O. 925, c/o Postmaster, San Francisco, California.* "You will notice the change in address. Use it for faster mail service. It seems my address is always changing. There is some Jap music on the radio. It is that weird five note oriental music that is so very monotonous. Once in awhile they give news for our benefit. Their exaggerated claims are very amusing. If they were correct we would have been beaten long ago."

* * * *

September 18, 1944: "My two hut mates and I just finished trying to play a trio on tonette ocarinas. It was a very poor attempt and wasn't especially appreciated by the men next door. It might be that they don't appreciate good music, huh?"

* * * *

September 20, 1944: "I'm enclosing two pictures captured from the Japs. They were taken on the island before we captured it. The one with three Japs (standing) and three Javenese laborers (squatting). The background shows that this place was once quite pretty before the invasion. The other is a Jap pilot by his bomber. He was an officer (see his sword). All these men are dead now and the trees, buildings and bomber destroyed."

* * * *

September 22, 1944: "We've been busy the last few days and will be occupied a few more. I'll not be able to write letters for a few days. Be patient, darling. I've been interrupted and just got back. We just had a staff meeting of officers. There were a few details to discuss about … well, that's a military secret."

* * * *

September 25, 1944: "I'm sitting here in the ward room, a guest of the Navy. I'm trying to write as the ship rocks. It is pleasant and cozy in here while outside it is raining and blowing. It is a swell night to be indoors. I've spent the day rather lazily, slept until 7 a.m., ate breakfast, walked around the deck, read an Ellery Queen mystery, and talked with whomever was in a conversational mood. I met some navy officers and had some interesting talk comparing life in the army and navy.

"This afternoon a couple navy officers asked me to go ashore with them. We took a small boat and went in to a beach. The rough water gave us a bit of spray to dodge, but we stayed reasonably dry. It took the men most of the afternoon to finish their business, so we didn't get back until nearly supper time.

"This is the life. We have very little to do, a good bunk to sleep in, good food to eat, hot water to wash in, a shower, and flush toilets. This is luxury, no less. It is good to rest now for we have had and will have a lot of hard days to make up for this."

* * * *

September 28, 1944: "I am still rocking and rolling and trying to write. About all we've been doing for several days is sleeping, eating, and reading. I've read several books. Now I'm reading *A Tree Grows in Brooklyn*."

* * * *

September 29, 1944: "We just finished supper. It is nice to eat off china plates with real silverware again. Makes a man feel almost civilized. We've been able to follow the war news pretty good aboard ship. They get daily radio reports and make typewritten summaries." *Lyle was on a ship, an LST en route to the island of Morotai.*

* * * *

October 2, 1944: "We arrived at our destination … and landed without opposition. We've been busy setting up a camp area and getting ready to operate. Our camp site is a jungle, so we had to clear out bush and dense undergrowth before we put up our tents. This place is as hot as all the rest. At least we have our seasons right again. It is fall here now. Soon we'll have the monsoons. I dread that a lot."

* * * *

October 3, 1944: "Today is our day for celebration and here we are thousands of miles apart and very lonely. Even though we have not yet spent an anniversary together these two years have been fuller and happier just to have you for my wife. Did you get the flowers ok? I think I ordered them far enough ahead.

"Our camp area is coming along pretty well. We are using poles to build frames for tents for all our installations. The mess hall, latrines, orderly rooms, dispensary, supply, showers, and a well are all taking form right now. It is hard and hot work but worth the effort in the little comfort they provide.

"Tonight is clear and hot. Soon it will be dark and a big tropical moon will be out. It is really a beautiful moon, but to us it is unwelcome for it quite often brings visits from the Nip air force. We have no lights in our tents yet so everyone has to go to bed early. It is too hot to sleep but toward morning it cools off to be pleasant enough."

* * * *

October 6, 1944: "I received the first of your letters at our new station this morning. It was the one of Sept. 8th written from Granite. I see Mom was keeping you busy with sewing, etc.

"There is a new plan in effect concerning return to the States. A man can take a choice of returning for a 30 day leave (exclusive of travel time) after 18 months of service and then returning to his unit until such time as the Army sees fit to relieve him after the war, or the alternative of waiting until he can go home by rotation (the time now is approximately 30 months (but will get shorter, I'm quite sure). Going home by rotation one gets a 21 day leave and then is sent to a replacement center for reassignment to another outfit. If that outfit is sent overseas he has to go with them. In other words rotation is going home and starting all over again.

"Both plans have their advantages depending entirely on a lot of unpredictable circumstances. Maybe in three or four months when my 18 months are up the overall picture will have changed so it will be easier to pick the best alternative. What do you think about the plans, honey?"

* * * *

October 8, 1944: "Today I stuck pretty close to the office. There were a couple of places I might have gone, but I'm so sore from riding my jeep over terrible roads that I'm glad to stay in one place. We've been trying to dig a well to get water for showers. The men are down about 30 feet and still no water. Now we have to haul in water in a truck. The limited amount doesn't give very adequate showers."

* * * *

October 9, 1944: "Today we had a little extra time to fix up our quarters. We built some shelves for our belongings and rigged some curtains to keep the rain from blowing in."

* * * *

October 11, 1944: "Somewhere in the Netherlands East Indies. *(Morotai)* You might have noticed that I can now give my location to some extent. I was sorry to hear of Grandma Young's death. It was a shock, but not a surprise for I've expected it for some time. Her life for the last few years was trying. Now she has peace for the next life. I hope Dad didn't take it too hard.

"I have missed another event in the life of our baby. I know how thrilled you must have been to have her take her first steps. Like most of her accomplishments she has learned this early. That proves she's a remarkable little girl. I had three letters from Mom today. She told me a few of the amusing things baby had done while you were visiting in Granite.

"Our work goes on about the same with a few flashes of excitement. Not long ago we saw a Jap plane destroyed. When it came over our anti-aircraft guns threw everything but the kitchen sink at it. It looked like a massive fireworks show. The Nip plane literally disappeared in mid-air. Pieces flew all over. Our raids from the Nips are quite ineffective. With foxholes for protection we have little to worry about. Everyone takes the raids in stride, but no one is careless. Now, honey, don't worry. These raids are so minor that I don't think I've even mentioned them before.

"If our quarters at the last station needed a woman's touch you should see our quarters now. Lumber isn't available here so we built a frame of logs and covered it with tin. It is adequate but far from homey. They are playing a new song on the phonograph, 'You gotta hug him in the morning, kiss him at night, give him plenty lovin' for a good man's hard to find'. That's how I want to be treated when I get home.

"This place is awful for the dust. One can hardly see ten feet in front of his vehicle on the roads. It is a red dust that hangs on everything and gives a peculiar appearance. In the evenings everyone is caked with the stuff so the shower is the most popular place in the Squadron. In this part of the world it is either dust or mud.

"Some of the men have found bananas growing around here. They are green but by picking and keeping them in a dark, damp place they ripen. They sure taste good after not having any for so long."

* * * *

October 16, 1944: "Thank you for the swell birthday card. It arrived a few days ago but I waited to open it until today. I am anxiously awaiting the package, and thank you for the subscription to *Reader's Digest.* I've got a quarter century to my credit. It makes me feel a little old, but I am satisfied with my position. There are few men 25 (years old) that have their health, education, money in the bank, and a wonderful wife and daughter. If only the war were over so we could start life together.

"Work is down to a routine again with us serving our purpose of maintaining airplanes. Everyone is more satisfied when they are working normally. The days go by much faster.

"I am sitting in my office near the airstrip. Planes are flying overhead, landing and taking off. Bulldozers are right outside my office clearing out the jungle. On the road trucks and jeeps are crawling along in a cloud of dust. In the other end of the building some men are hammering away on a bench they are making. It is quite exciting. It would be fun to point out all the operations to you."

* * * *

October 19, 1944: "You ask how I voted in the elections. I voted a straight Republican ticket. In State government there isn't the slightest doubt in my mind that the Republicans have given much better government than those before them. As for the Federal government I think there is time for a change. The government has bungled too many things and have had a total disregard for thrift. Dewey may be inexperienced but he is a practical man and has shown that he will surround himself with a brilliant staff so as to operate efficiently. The largest part of the next term will be in a state of peace. It is the home policy of the Democrats that I have never liked. What are your opinions?

"I guess we should be excited tonight. The Allied landings in the Philippines is a climax to our operations over the last 16 months. From Milne Bay in New Guinea to the new beach head is 2500 miles. It sounds like we have covered a lot of territory and I guess we have.

"A few minutes ago a Navy Ensign walked in looking for an airplane part. He introduced himself and we struck up a conversation. His name was Johnson and his brogue was Swedish, so with a 50-50 chance I asked him if he was from Minnesota. Score 1. He later mentioned a room mate so I asked him if he went to the University. Score 2. We began to talk of classes and I mentioned my wife was in the class of '41, also. (I really was in the class of 1942.) He asked what your name was. Swenson, Marguerite Swenson. Yes. Well, I'll be darned. It seems he was active in L.S.A. also and remembers a lot of our acquaintances. His name is Ervin or Erwin. Do you remember him? He's built heavy like me and has red hair and a reddish complexion. I'm going over to visit him in a few days, and we are going to talk over old times. He's doing the same type of work as I am, only on Navy planes."

* * * *

October 23, 1944: "Our camp is in good shape now. I think it is about the best we have ever had. No one has floors in their tents, but they are still rather neat and comfortable. The straight slender trees in the surrounding jungle have been put to use for our tent frames. Our well never did come through, but we are able to haul enough for skimpy showers. It is amazing how little water a man uses for a bath when it is rationed.

"I'm enclosing a proclamation from General MacArthur's Hq. to the people of the Philippines and a flag dual American and Philippine. These leaflets were dropped on the Islands at the time of the invasion."

* * * *

October 26, 1944: "Today has been a big day in the Pacific War. Our Navy and Air Force have been busy fighting three groups of the enemy fleet. The reports so far have been encouraging. Quite a number of enemy warships have been sunk or damaged in the Philippine Islands. The full story will not be available until the action is over.

(We know now that this was the battle of Leyte Gulf, called the world's greatest sea battle which took place October 23, 24, and 25th, 1944)

"One of the officers got hold of a bunch of 'sweet potatoes' (ocarinas), and we have played them until we have almost driven everyone nuts. I've even gotten tired of my own playing which shows the extent of their unpopularity with me. Now it is afternoon. This noon I got shots for typhoid and cholera. My blood should be about half serum and the rest white corpuscles when the army gets through with me."

* * * *

October 29, 1944: "We had a couple of real treats last night. We were able to get some PX supplies and each man was permitted to buy 5 Milky Way bars and a package of cookies. The candy was rather gooey, but tasted very good. It isn't often we get candy and cookies. The other treat was the show, 'In Society', with

Abbott and Costello. They were their own silly selves, but we enjoyed the picture in spite of its slapstick.

"I have some nylon from a salvaged parachute that I'll try to send you one of these days. It could be made into a blouse or something. The paper container (Jap) in the box was a carton containing Nip rifle cartridges.

"I am thrilled that Lois Marie says 'dada' and likes my picture. Maybe she realizes a bit that she has a father. She will know soon enough when we meet for the first time, for she will get a lot of attention from me.

"The weather here is the most unpredictable I've ever seen. If I were to forecast this part of the world it would have to go something like this: 'Weather for tomorrow, breezes, winds, gales from the southwest and northeast probably shifting to northwest and southeast. Cloudy and fair if not warmer. Barometric pressure shilly shally. Snow, sleet, and hail not likely.' The only thing I'm sure of is that there will be plenty of it."

* * * *

November 9, 1944: "Happy birthday, little one. Daddy is sorry he can't be with you to see those eyes sparkle at the sight of the single candle on your cake and the gifts you will receive. To you the day will not mean anything, but Mommy and Daddy realize the significance. You've been in our family a year now. How do you like it?

"I hear by the radio that Roosevelt has been elected again. I'm sorry to hear it, but now that he is we'll support him to the best of our ability. The main thing is to get this mess over with and to get through the post war period of readjustment as quickly as possible.

"We've heard quite a bit about the conflict between returning overseas veterans and civilians. Both are somewhat at fault. The civilians can't realize the sacrifice that the veterans have made. The men over here will find it hard to forget and will resent the civilian ingratitude. As far as I'm concerned I'm glad those in the States can live much as they have always and have few sacrifices materially. It saves us over here a lot of worry about those loved ones at home. It is the civilian who says, 'If the war lasts two more years, I'll be well-fixed, that starts me burning.' I will try not to be bitter about the war. It is bad enough as is without letting its effects carry on afterwards. Thank God for the marvelous support and hard hours of work that all but a few have contributed on the home front."

* * * *

November 12, 1944: "I'm sorry that I can't save every one of your sweet letters. I keep them for a couple of months and then when the pile gets too big for the corner of my footlocker I must throw them away. Because of our frequent moves I must conserve all the space possible. Today was one of those bad days. I read them all over carefully, and then ..."

* * * *

November 23, 1944: "For the last couple days I've been very busy working night and day. This morning I have a little time, but I expect to be busy again this afternoon. Darling, don't worry about me if you don't get mail for a week or more. I'll write whenever I can, you can be sure."

* * * *

November 24-27, 1944: Somewhere in the Pacific. "The sea is calm and very blue with light swells. Above the sky is studded with fluffs of white clouds. The ship glides smoothly through the water with only the subtle throb of its engines to indicate that the ship isn't standing still. You would enjoy the atmosphere, darling, or better we'd enjoy it together. Life aboard is rather nice. I share a room with other officers. It is crowded but comfortable. The meals aboard are always a treat. Not only is the food good, but the idea of sitting down to a table with a real cloth, real china and silver is pleasing. Unfortunately, the men aren't living as well, but their ingenuity has resulted in some makeshift but adequate shelters on deck. Thanksgiving Day went by unnoticed here, but I guess it was Nov. 23rd.

"Yesterday some natives came along side in their outrigger canoes and dived for coins and cigarettes that the men threw to them. Most of them were small boys and they were having a big time. The natives here are brown-skinned and better looking than others we have seen. They are quite intelligent and clean."

* * * *

November 30, 1944: "I have a chance to mail this now so will rush it off. I'll write again in a couple of days."

* * * *

December 2, 1944: Somewhere in the Philippines. "I'm sorry about the scarcity of letters lately, but I think you understand. We are only partly set up. Our shelter is whatever we can find or chisel out and is inadequate to keep off the almost steady rains. I've been sleeping with wet blankets for three nights and there doesn't seem to be any relief in sight. In contrast to our poor living conditions the food is swell. This morning we had fresh eggs and this noon we'll have chicken, yes chicken! We missed out on our Thanksgiving rations so are getting them now."

(Lyle was on the island of Leyte, and the dating on his letters tell that he was there about five weeks, until about the 8th of January, 1945:)

"The Philippines are quite interesting. There are a few towns which are quite crude, but a good deal more civilization than we've seen in a long time. Most of the towns were evacuated during the Jap occupation, the people preferring the discomforts of the mountains to the brutality of the Nips. The towns are therefore in need of repair. The natives, or I should say civilians, for they don't like to be called natives, live in houses built of bamboo with thatched roofs. A few of the more well-to-do have lumber houses. Each little town has a church as its largest and best building.

"The churches are of the old Spanish Mission type and are quite colorful. Each town also has a one-room school house and a few small shops. The shops have little to sell now, but will probably do better after a longer period of American occupation.

"The civilians are small brown people with quite nice features. They greatly resemble the American Indians. They are allowed to roam freely through our areas and do quite a good business selling souvenirs, doing laundry and helping with tasks of all kinds. They are all quite clean but poorly dressed. They have some admirable qualities that I've particularly noticed. They are friendly, appreciative, courteous and honest. Most are rather shy, but can be brought into conversation with a little tact. Most speak English fairly well, well enough to trade and tell us how badly the Japs treated them.

"The Japs abused their women, forced men into labor gangs, killed without reason, burned their homes, stole their food and inflicted almost any kind of brutal treatment they could think of. The Philippinos are all very happy with their liberation and try to show their appreciation."

* * * *

December 3, 1944: "How is our little princess? When I see all the little Philippino children running around I am reminded of our little girl. I'm oh so eager to see our little Lois Marie.

"We are undergoing a monetary change again. This time we use the Philippine peso (50 cents) and a centavo (one-half cent). I have four kinds of money in my pocket book now: Australian pound, Dutch guilder, American dollars and Philippine pesos. I also have some bills the Japs used here. They forced people to accept this money in exchange for their possessions. Now the money is useless except for what the people get for its souvenir value. I'm sending three of these Jap invasion notes.

"This morning I had my laundry done by a Philippino. They wash clothes in a stream near here. Their work is quite good and inexpensive. It is a relief not to worry about washing clothes anymore. I always hated the job.

"Today it isn't raining and everyone is getting their property dried out. We have some tents now, so will be fairly well set up by tonight. The men feel a lot better now that we have some shelter. We have facilities for only two meals a day now, and I sure get hungry between meals.

"Our area is located right on a nice beach. I think I'll find time to take a swim every day. Remember the fun we had with the breakers on the beach in Venice. Five little children just entered our tent. They are jabbering away 'to beat the cars'. They all have Spanish names like Dominic, Manuela, etc. The Philippinos certainly are prolific, for there seem to be five or more children in every family."

* * * *

December 4, 1944: "I went into a little town here last night and visited the mayor. He was a middle-aged man who spoke excellent English. I made arrangements with him to furnish about a dozen laborers to work for us. I might tell you about his house. It was a frame building of one story built about 8 feet off the ground. There were three rooms with woven grass walls. They had four wooden chairs and a small table. There were an abundance of grass mats on the floor and several grass baskets about. The mayor's wife was very courteous, but stayed outside the ring of conversation. I wish you could have shared the experience."

* * * *

December 5, 1944: "This is one of the nicest days I've seen in a long time. There is a cool breeze blowing in off the bay and even in the sun it isn't too hot. Now that we are further north I suppose we can expect cooler weather. We have close contact with the civilians. We often have whole families go through the area and stop to talk and trade. The people all look younger than they probably are because they are so small. One woman told me last night that she had seven children.

"The people dress fairly well considering their long oppression by the Nips. The men wear shirts with either shorts or pants and hats of either felt or straw. The women wear very simple dresses with no belts or frills. The children wear little slipovers like undershirts made from hemp. Often the garment is too short to accomplish its purpose. No one wears shoes. I am told that almost every home has a sewing machine. The Singer Co. must have had a darn good salesman in these parts before the war."

* * * *

December 7, 1944: "A little boy and girl came into our tent this morning. We asked them a few questions which they shyly answered while eyeing some gum I had out on my ration box. When I gave them each a stick, away they went, mission accomplished. I think the Philippino kids are cute and well mannered. With all the civilians roaming around the camp area no one has had a thing stolen. They might be shrewd traders, but they will not steal.

"Just now a woman stuck her head in the tent and asked if I have any laundry. They make pretty good money washing clothes. The Philippine president has set a standard price which is reasonable. The women wash our clothes in streams by beating them with a flat paddle. Some of them have earned enough money so that they come around and try to buy towels."

* * * *

December 8, 1944: "Lt. Bowerman, with whom I share a two-man tent, is sitting across from me on a cot also writing to his wife. He's an Oklahoman. Our tent is new, quite comfortable and doesn't leak. The ground here is sandy so the rain doesn't bother us much by making it muddy. I just got the news tonight. Nineteen Nip ships were sunk yesterday in the Philippine operations. The Nips keep trying to reinforce their troops, but we are making it very expensive for them."

* * * *

December 10, 1944: The news release last night told of an earthquake that rocked Japan on the third anniversary of Pearl Harbor.

"Did I tell you that I have a valet now, or should I say, 'No. 1 boy'. He is a Philippine boy about 18 of higher than average intelligence. During the Jap occupation he was with the guerillas fighting in the hills. His name is Felix, but prefers to be called Feely. He does all kinds of chores and is especially valuable for contact with the civilians. His services are very inexpensive, and he is very devoted and eager. I'll try to send a picture of him sometime."

* * * *

December 11, 1944: "Today I had time to walk into the village near our camp area. The army has moved in to spoil the atmosphere. The olive drab of the army tents, vehicles, and guns are scattered among the grass huts of the civilians. Even with the army there one can imagine the village as it must be in normal times. The houses are arranged in blocks each with a little yard in which there are shrubs, banana and coconut trees, etc., which cover the whole property with shade. The houses have only openings for windows and doors, and the walls and floors are covered with straw woven mats of various designs and colors. The men sit around and smoke while the women pound rice into flour, pound coconuts into tuba (the native wine), or weave grass into baskets, mats and hats. The children romp all over the place having a big time. One Philippino told me that one reason for all the children is that they kept their women pregnant during the Jap occupation because the Japs did not attack a pregnant woman as readily.

"Lt. Bowerman and I just finished making fudge from chocolate pudding, condensed milk and some butter. I'm doubtful how good it will taste, but we get very hungry for candy. I'd ask you to send candy once in awhile, but most of it is spoiled before it gets here. It's been three weeks since I've had any mail now. I've had to be content with reading over your old letters. Darling, those letters are very precious to me. I am grateful for your faithfulness in writing."

* * * *

December 13, 1944: "How I wish I could be home with you and baby now. We'd be planning for Christmas and having so much fun. We haven't had a real Christmas yet, have we? I am confident that next year we will be together.

"We've been bothered very little with air raids lately. Thank God. It is a relief for I have already had my share of foxhole time eating dirt and praying, too. The man that said, 'There are no atheists foxholes' knew what he was saying. You often hear that the Air Corps never sees action, but that's false. We've seen our share of the war. We have had very few casualties though in our outfit.

"Lois Marie is a chubby little rascal. In the pictures she looks bright-eyed and a little mischievous. Is she? I hope that we are not long in getting acquainted when I come home."

* * * *

December 16, 1944: "This is the first time I've had to write in a couple of days. I've been fairly busy. I worked 41 hours straight through and have just now caught up on sleep. It wasn't physical labor, but even standing around, walking, and giving orders is tiresome in a long stretch. I've been Beach Officer for unloading a couple of ships. Barges bring the cargo to the beach, and it was my job to see that it was unloaded as soon as possible. The beach is too soft for trucks and nearly every one has to be winched out or pulled out with a caterpillar tractor. It seems that a good part of my overall job in the army has been handling heavy equipment.

"The news continues to be good in this theater. The B-29 raids on Japan are heartening. Last night we learned of a 1000 ton raid on the Nips principal aircraft factory. The length of the war over here will depend on how long the Nips will fight before accepting unconditional surrender. They know they are beaten, but are fanatical enough to fight to the last man."

* * * *

December 22, 1944: "Darling, I hope the mail comes through soon. It has been almost a month now since I received your last letter. It is hard to keep up my morale without your letters to cheer me. Take good care of yourself and baby. You mean everything to me."

* * * *

December 24, 1944: "Christmas is not just another day after all. Two of your letters came today, the first in a month. Never have two letters meant so much to me. I am glad you accomplished your Christmas shopping so effectively. The gifts you have picked are swell and will be appreciated. I hope you have a nice Christmas with the all the family participating. I miss the spirit of friendliness, good will and cheer that goes with all the social life among the Scandinavians. I would have given anything to see Lois Marie's enthusiasm over the whole affair. I can imagine how big and bright those blue eyes where when she received her gifts."

* * * *

Christmas Day, 1944: "The Army has done well to make our day here as good as possible. We have only worked at the absolute necessities. Everyone has had a day of leisure. We had turkey for dinner with real white potatoes. We also received an issue of beer. As much as these things are appreciated, the most important thing to me was the two letters that came yesterday. I've lost count of the number of times I've read them and drifted into dreams of my girls and home."

* * * *

December 27, 1944: "I'm a lucky guy when I can get three of your letters in one day. At last the mail is catching up. The two pictures of the baby are precious. She is getting prettier with each picture you send. I am proud to show these pictures to all my friends. There is no man prouder of his wife and baby that I. My pictures are my most precious possessions over here for nothing other than letters can strengthen my morale so effectively."

* * * *

December 28, 1944: "The mail orderly brought two V-mail letters today. They have been slower than air mail in the last month or so. These were of Nov. 28th and Dec. 4th. They were sure swell letters putting me in the usual good mood. I carved this letter opener for you from mahogany which grew in abundance at our last station. I hope you like it. Since you wrote I see the sixth war bond drive went way over the top. I'm glad we contributed our share. Dad S. has been surely doing a swell job holding the chairman's job continuously. With that and all the work he and Gordon have been doing on the farm they've more than contributed their share to the war effort."

* * * *

December 31, 1944: "Happy New Year. Old man '44 will soon be gone and I can't say I'm sorry. It has been a lonely year lacking in the happiness that would have been if we had been together. Sometime within 1945 I'm confident I'll be home. Keep up your brave endurance of this loneliness a little longer, darling, like the good soldier you've been. Today your Christmas package came. It was a swell selection of things I need. Everything came through in excellent condition. The candy is very good and tonight Lt. Bowerman and I will eat the olives. The pen works fine as you can see. My old one wouldn't hold ink any more and had to be dipped and even the point was getting scratchy. Thank you so much, Sweetheart. I've finished the book by Ogden Nash. I haven't enjoyed anything so much in a long time. Did you read it before you sent it? It wasn't full of laughs, but was packed with chuckles."

The Philippines: 1944–45

Philippinos met our boat in their outrigger canoe. They were selling souvenirs.

Philippine home constructed of bamboo with palm fronds woven together. Houses were quite cool.

Pilots named their planes. Here "Putt-Putt" is being repaired by Lyle's squadron. Note number of missions marked on the side.

Philippine President Sergio Osmena. Lyle enjoyed meeting this charming man with other soldiers during a two-day leave to Leyte in March 1945.

Tech Sergeant Carl Dietz (OH) and Staff Sergeant Marko deRusso (NY) purchase chickens for a supper on Mindoro.

March 1945: Standing: Staff Sergeant Thomas (OH), Sergeant Liley (IL), Staff Sergeant Syme (MN), Master Sergeant MacFee (WV)
Kneeling: Sergeant Godsey (KY), Captain Lyle Young (MN) Tech Sergeant Schoenbarum (NY)

1945

January 6, 1945: 336th Service Squadron, A.P.O. 321, c/o Postmaster, San Francisco, California. Somewhere in the Philippines. "Somewhere Else. Here I am again rocking and rolling with the Navy to new adventures and experiences. I'm enjoying the trip as usual with the luxuries of hot water, beds with sheets, and good food served with silverware and plates. I've been sleeping a lot to make up for two days of continuous work before we embarked." *This was a trip to Mindoro in the Philippines. Jap planes often shot at their ship, but the American anti-aircraft shot them down.*

* * * *

January 9, 1945: "I am very happy tonight. Five letters of November 15, 16, 20, and December 18 and 20 came today. They mean so much to me now when we cannot be together. Today we accomplished a lot toward getting set up for operation. We used a couple of bulldozers to level off the area and then staked out the spaces for our shops, offices, etc., Lumber is almost non-existent here, and even straight trees for poles are few so the construction of our installations is going to be difficult.

"There is a little railroad which the army has put to good use. The cars look like toys compared to the ones at home. This place was once a sugar plantation and the railroad was used to haul the cane. There are quite a number of warehouses and factory buildings around to indicate a big industry."

* * * *

January 11, 1945: "Here is your foreign correspondent again with today's news. Today it was necessary to do a lot of driving over very rough and dusty roads. I was scouting around for lumber, tents, etc., to get our buildings in line. I managed to do fairly well. This afternoon I had to go to a meeting to discuss operating plans and policies. Nothing I didn't already know. I ran into Capt. Schilling. He's in a Service Squadron near here, still the same old Schilling, cheerful and easy going. He asked about you and Lois Marie.

"I picked up some Philippino guerillas along the road today. They were pretty shabby and battle worn. They have had a tough time the last few years and are impressed with the big way the Yanks do things. Our equipment enables us to do things in a hurry, even surprises me once in awhile when I see a good job being done.

"My tent mates are building some furniture out of old crates. It brought up a discussion of furniture and a statement by Lt. Bowerman, 'There's one thing I don't like and that's twin beds'." I told him I thought they were ok, for it is always nice to have a spare bed in the house. Huh?

"We had a hectic night with a tent that does little more than strain the water. In choosing a tent it was impossible to tell if it would leak or not, and so at the first rain one finds out how lucky they are. It started to rain about 11 p.m. Almost spontaneously all three of us jumped out of bed and began stumbling around in the dark trying to rig up some kind of secondary shelter over the beds. This shelter composed of towels, scraps of canvas, waterproof paper and a host of other things was a weird sight when we got up this morning. Of course, we all had to make uncomplimentary remarks about the horrible looking arrangement of the other's beds … Right now we are working on four different kinds of aircraft. That complicates things a little, but the men are versatile enough to take care of the job."

* * * *

January 13, 1945: "After work we went to get some poles and began to construct a frame to build a hut. This tent is impossible, so we are anxious to get a dry home. Our new home will be 12' by 20' with a canvas roof and chicken wire sides."

* * * *

January 14, 1945: "Today we put the tarp on the roof of our tent. It was a very heavy canvas to wrestle around and took the three of us a couple of hours. A few more hours and we'll be ready to move in. Again we found a Philippino to do our laundry, so I have that problem solved. The population here is so small that I was afraid I'd have to put up with 'blue Mondays' again. I had three suits of khakis and a lot of other pieces done for one peso (50 cents), so you can see they are most reasonable.

"My chief clerk is sick in the hospital, so that handicaps the work a little. He had the initiative to take care of most details without being told and is a valuable man to me. I intend to visit him tomorrow to see his condition.

"A colonel just walked in to get the correct nomenclature and stock numbers on some flying clothing. The Air Corps has some beautiful leather jackets that are issued to pilots only, so that he will have to use every bit of his rank to get this requisition through. A guy can never tell who will walk in to see you. As a rule I'm not disturbed by a lot of rank. Even had a two-star general walk in one day."

"By the way, what's our financial situation now? It is a nice thing to have a couple thousand dollars saved. The average family only earns about $2000 a year and we have saved that in a little over a year. We have your folks to thank for that. I'd like to get them a real swell gift in appreciation for all they've done."

* * * *

January 18, 1945: "Today we strung up the camouflage netting on the sides of our shack. We've done about all we can, and it is certainly comfortable for over here. Our cots are covered with a mosquito bar and the table is cluttered with junk. It is still comparatively neat. Our chow is pretty good. We've had fresh meat quite often. Yesterday we had pork for the first time in months. It was delicious, but I hadn't had it for so long it make me sick. Guess it was too rich.

"It has been a disagreeable day. There has been a high wind all day blowing dust all over. It is very much like the dust storms we had during the drought years at home. A lot of our tents blew down and we've had to work to keep the rest of them up. Now the wind has died down so I guess the storm is over. The leg that I hurt a couple weeks ago is fully recovered now. I'm feeling healthy as ever. Your old man is bearing up pretty well under the trials of war. The mail service is slower than an anemic earthworm with bunions. It has been several days now since we've had mail. Those all important letters will come in a bunch, I guess.

"I got a real hunk of morale today. Three Vs and an airmail came ranging in dates from Nov. 14 to Jan. 3rd. You kind of woke me up when you stated that both Gordon and Jean might be married when I return. The prospect of Gordon getting married doesn't seem strange to me, but I have trouble imagining Jean as anything but a little girl yet. Did I tell you I'm carving a miniature of a Philippino going to a cock fight. I have it almost done and will send it to you.

"Have I told you about the cock fights? The men who own roosters tie sharp little knives to the legs of the two contestants. Then the cocks are placed in a large ring and they fight until one is dead or leaves the ring. Every Sunday there are these fights in the villages attended by large crowds with a lot of betting. It is a rather cruel sport.

"On our maps Glenn and I are following very closely the rapid Russian advance. We are stretching our hopes that they will continue until Germany folds. Then we shall go to Tokyo. Not until Germany is defeated can we expect any rotation or leave plan to work over here. There are some men over here who aren't so terribly anxious to go home. They miss good food, drinks, women, etc., but there is nothing as strong as my reason for wanting to return, you and Lois Marie. When we meet in Minneapolis I'd like to meet you alone for a day or two before going to our homes.

"We have been able to get quite a bit of lumber here so that our mess hall, showers, latrines, dispensary are the best we have had yet. Headquarters has been strict on the army rule of distinction between officers and enlisted men, so we officers have our own separate shower, dining room, and latrine for the first time. Before we've tried to live as much like the men as possible."

* * * *

January 27, 1945: "All of your old letters have been coming in the last few days. Today yours of Nov. 26th came. Old or new every letter is wonderful. If I should ever get to Guam I will look up the grave of Oscar Holmquist (my cousin). I would like to be of comfort to his family. The cemeteries I have seen over here are very neat, clean and kept up very well.

"Can't kick about this place. One of the nicest features is 'no raids'. It is nice not to be shocked out of bed with those three shots during the night. Last night the men in the Squadron had a rat killing contest. They armed themselves with clubs and flashlights and prowled around the area. The evening's total was 114. The rats here are almost as numerous as the ants. Between them they make it extremely difficult to keep food safe from their prowling."

* * * *

February 6, 1945: "We all feel pretty good about the liberation of Manila. We knew the news quite awhile before you did, for once. I hope to get to see the city some time."

* * * *

February 8, 1945: "Today was different in that we had a hard rain. It poured down for over an hour trying to make up for the week of dry weather we'd had. I got caught in the middle of it in a jeep without a top. I went through a large puddle and the jeep drowned out. There I sat in a big puddle in a pouring rain. There was nothing to do but relax and try to enjoy the rain. After the rain there was a large, bright rainbow, the promise in the sky.

"Our set up on the line is really looking spiffy now. Everything is neat and efficient. Each shop has a mobile truck or a portable building so that when we move we'll have little difficulty in tearing down and setting up. I've stressed mobility for a long time and have finally got things like I want."

* * * *

February 10, 1945: "Here are the pictures you've often asked about. They have been several months getting here. The package was wet and moldy, but I was able to salvage most of it. I cut off most of the mold on the large one and tried to shade in the rest with pencil. You can frame the small one, if you like, and use the large one to scare the mice out of the basement." *(These were great pictures he had taken in MacKay.)*

"Finally got the Christmas package from folks S., so I wrote them instead of you last night. The last few days have really been busy. We can't get all the work done in the day so we've had to put in a lot of night work. I've also had to cancel days off until things slow down again. A good part of the work has been receiving and indexing airplane parts. We've also shipped a lot of stuff out. All this has been in addition to regular work. I find now that tomorrow we have an inspection."

* * * *

February 12, 1945: "A colonel and captain came to visit and we went to the mess hall for a real treat. We had corn on the cob with real butter, the first time in a couple of years. The Philippinos grow corn somewhere near here. The colonel has 36 months overseas so is expecting to go home soon.

"I'm enclosing a picture of the P-38 that an acquaintance of my flies. As you can see, he's doing well with 26 Nips to his credit. We've worked on his plane once in awhile and felt pride in our work. The P-38 Lightning is a beautiful plane, one of the smoothest and most graceful of them all. It has served well in this theater.

"Glenn and I just finished cutting up some leather we got. We are going to see if we can make some jackets. Don't laugh, at least not yet. It is dubious how good a job we can do, but we'll try. Our parachute shop has a heavy duty sewing machine we can use. I've never tried to sew anything before, but I've watched you and Mom, so I've got some ideas about how to proceed. We cut up an old shirt to get a pattern for the front, back and sleeves, and will improvise from there."

* * * *

February 18, 1945: "Things look pretty good, don't they? The news of the Naval Task Force hitting Japan is particularly encouraging. I never thought it possible to do that this early. I also read of paratroopers landing on Corregidor, and of the Jap claims that we have invaded Iwo Jima. That is unconfirmed as yet by our side. We are slowly getting into position to start the big phase of the war over here. I'm now authorized to wear the Philippine liberation ribbon with a bronze star. That makes two with the Asiatic Pacific ribbon. I think we may get one for the Netherlands East Indies too. On my sleeve I can now wear three overseas bars and soon will have a hash mark for three years.

"This afternoon I sewed on the jacket. It was the first time I'd used a sewing machine so all the seams aren't so straight, but not too bad either. I still have to sew the collar and bottom. It is going to be a simple drape shape job. If the thing turns out all right will you put a lining in it for me?

"Tonight the officers played volley ball for an hour. Doc and I played against Mason, Herman, and Bowerman. We didn't keep score. We are going to play often as we all need some physical exercise. The ankle I hurt at the last station bothers me a little when I use it a lot. By playing volley ball I'll be able to strengthen it again.

"I found this certificate showing me to be a member of the Ancient Order of the Deep, a full-fledged 'Trusty Shellback'. It was awarded with due ceremony and initiation when we crossed the equator."

* * * *

February 25, 1945: "I hope you have a pleasant birthday. Did the floral greeting arrive ok? *Lyle often ordered fresh flowers delivered from the florist in Montevideo.* Tonight also marks 19 months overseas.

"Today I decided to put a floor in a hut we officers use for a meeting place. It was quite a job as the lumber was wet, warped, crooked and cracked. Somehow I got it to fit fairly well with just enough convenient cracks to dispose of cigarette butts."

* * * *

March 2, 1945: "I have met quite a few of the American prisoners of war that have been rescued. They are unhealthy looking. You cannot imagine the horrors they have endured under the barbarians. I've seen a man with all his fingers cut off because of some small infraction of a rule. I talked with a Philippino who had two daughters, 13 and 15, whom Japs kidnapped a couple of years ago as hostesses for their brothels. This poor father hasn't seen his daughters since. The stories of Jap atrocities are not exaggerated by any means.

"Just saw a rat run over my bed. They are really thick around here. They sound like a herd of elephants running around the shack at night. Our (mosquito) bars now keep out mosquitoes and rats. Handy things, huh?"

* * * *

March 5, 1945: "Last evening and this morning two women and a little boy stayed in one of our huts that we had vacated for them. They had just been released after three years of internment by the Japs. One woman was interned with her husband and three children. The other was a missionary nurse for the Lutheran church when she was captured. She was on her way to China before the war and trouble there caused her to be detained in the Philippines where she was captured after Pearl Harbor. Both ladies were very nice and overjoyed by their freedom. I took them down to the strip after dinner where they caught a plane back to the place where they will depart for the States. There were a lot of Minnesota people in their group, they said.

"Just got your V-mail of Feb. 11th. You had written the letter from Betty's place in St. Paul. You had gone down with Gordon. It is swell that you can get out once in awhile by going into the cities to stay with Betty."

* * * *

March 9, 1945: "I have men working tonight all night. I'll have to go down to the strip after awhile to see how they are coming. I have a darn good T/Sgt. in charge so don't have to worry about the work getting done. I get nothing but the best respect and work from every one of my men. I'm sure proud of the swell way they respond to any task. The men working tonight worked all day and I had to call them out of a show, but there wasn't a kick from any one. With more like them the war would be over now.

"Sometimes I get quite bitter about all the men who are still in the States. Over half our army is still there. When some men do get home they are sent right back overseas. I know a Sgt. who went home after 33 months and after his leave was sent right back over here. Why couldn't he take a U.S.O. Commando's job and let someone else sweat it out overseas for awhile. Such is the army. I hope that when I come home I can stay in the States."

* * * *

March 10, 1945: *336th Air Service Squadron, A.P.O. 321, c/o Postmaster, San Francisco, California.* "Note a small change in my address. We are now the 336th Air Service Squadron. It is a change in name only. I bought a poncho today and just in time. The quartermaster has a sales commissary here from which we can buy any clothing we need. I'm getting awfully tired of wearing and seeing only olive drab clothing."

* * * *

March 11, 1945: "Did you notice the return address? Yes, it's Captain Young now. Today orders came through from General Mac Arthur's Headquarters authorizing me these lovely little 'railroad tracks'. I've been a Capt. now since March 2nd. This means a good sized pay raise for us. The amounts are about so: Base pay $200.00, 10% for overseas $20.00, Quarters $90.00, Rations for two $42.00. Total $352.00. Out of this comes my rations of $22.00 per month, insurance $6.60 per month, and of course, your allotment."

* * * *

March 12, 1945: "I guess I've shaken hands of every man in the outfit today. They've all been around to congratulate me. It isn't correct military procedure for an enlisted man to be so familiar with an officer, but over here a lot of those technicalities are ignored, thank goodness."

* * * *

March 15, 1945: *Again Lyle sent some house plans.* "Our house won't be very conventional, but it will be convenient and attractive and will suit us perfectly." *After owning a Dutch Colonial house in Minneapolis and a Ranch Style house in Lincoln, Lyle designed, with some ideas from me, the house of our dreams and we had it built in 1978. Yes, it did suit us perfectly.*

* * * *

March 16, 1945: "We had another inspection today. Everything was ok. I'm getting used to having inspections. We've sure had a bunch of them since we've been here. My promotion is the best indication that I've been doing ok on them. Next time when you go to the cities will you get me 4 Captain's bars, 4 Air Corps insignia and a couple of officer's U.S.s. I'll enclose a note to use in case they hesitate to sell them to you. Send them in letters and they'll get here quicker."

* * * *

March 17, 1945: "More pictures to make our album grow. Wish I could tell you the complete stories of each. If you look on the desk in the one picture of Pres. Osmena you'll see our Squadron picture that we gave him."

* * * *

March 21, 1945: "We had these two pictures taken of our office staff. The hut behind us is the office. It is kinda small for seven men to work in, but there are so many records to keep that I need that many."

* * * *

March 22, 1945: "I would like to attend your folks' silver wedding anniversary. That is a day for celebration. Today I saw Lt. Ray for about an hour. He's moving soon. We had a swell visit about our wives, the war, rotation, etc. He says he's been in for Captain, so I imagine he'll make it soon. I hope that someday after the war we can see all the friends we've made in our travels."

* * * *

March 23, 1945: "We are going to have to move our area to high ground before the rainy season. Because of my engineering experience I was picked to lay it out and supervise the building of it. Plans call for quite an elaborate layout with floors in every building. When it is finished it will be the best we have ever had.

"Tonight we had two Philippinos to supper. They were executives for a large sugar company who gave us a very interesting picture of the Nip occupation and business trends in the Philippines. He told me an engineer could make thousands of dollars in the Philippines after the war. No thanks."

* * * *

March 25, 1945: "Today I've done a little engineering work. I laid out the new camp area which is located on a hill. It was good to work with a transit, a slide rule, and trigonometry tables again. *(Lyle included a sketch of the layout.)* The men's tents are arranged on two circular curves set on a hillside so as to escape the winds that blow hard during the rainy season. There will be clubs for both the enlisted men and the officers.

"I'd like to have you knit me a light colored sleeveless V-neck sweater, the kind men wear with a sport coat. It is sweet of you to want to make something for me." *(The result was a pale yellow cable knit sleeveless V-neck sweater which he did not get until after our second daughter Crystal Ann was born in 1946, after his return.)*

* * * *

March 26, 1945: "Yesterday the second Christmas package from you arrived. The only items that weren't ok were the two rolls of candy which were melted. I'm wearing the slippers now, pleasant to wear after lugging around GI clodhoppers all day. Glenn, George, and I made quick work of the cookies. I wish you had heard the swell compliments on them. The towel, hair dressing, and soap are all good practical gifts.

"The men are singing some hillbilly songs. Someone has a guitar and is strumming along. Sometimes I like the slow monotony of that type of song. There are a lot of men from West Virginia and Kentucky who all know a lot of the old folk songs or ballads.

"We burned off our new area today. The wind was from a direction that allowed us to control the fire. Burning it off will help control the rats and ticks. I'll be glad to be back to a place that isn't infested with small life.

"Tonight is Saturday night but I don't think I'll go to town. Why? Cuz I 'ain't saw' a town in a couple of years. It will seem odd to get back to a city and see the bright lights, hurrying people, and hear car horns, laughter, policemen's whistles, etc., again. How I'd like to take you to a show, dance or just walk."

* * * *

April 1, 1945: "A little while ago we all had an argument on the relative merits of our own states. Each man in the army is a self-made Chamber of Commerce for his own state and town. No matter what is said, to every man his own state is still the best."

* * * *

April 2, 1945: "We have had to take over another Squadron's duties and so our work is doubled for awhile. The work is divided too, being several miles apart. A large number of complications have arisen already which we hope to have straightened out in a couple of days. A S/Sgt. was just in and informed me he is the father of a baby boy. He's been sweating out the word for over a month. I know exactly how he felt. That V-mail I received on November 29, 1943, was the most important letter I received. I'll always keep that letter." *(regarding Lois Marie's birth on November 9, 1943.)*

* * * *

April 10, 1945: "Last night my men and I had a little party. We had a lot of work to be accomplished so I had them work straight through until 7 p.m. In the afternoon I sent out some of the men to trade with the Philippines for some chickens. For the cloth of a parachute and a couple bars of soap they got quite a few fryers. We fried them and made some coffee and everyone had a big feast. There was some singing and a lot of talk to make the evening interesting. The men all had a good time."

* * * *

April 13, 1945: "Tonight I'm writing from our new area. We are located on a series of low rolling hills which are quite pretty. We are within walking distance of our work, a big advantage. All winter has been like summer in the Philippines, but now is getting even hotter. If I put on a clean uniform it is all wet and soiled within an hour. A person always feels sticky and dirty. Our daily shower is the high point of the day.

"I received your letter of Easter Sunday today. I'm happy my girls liked their corsages. I shall be anxious to get the pictures Mother took that day. *(Lyle had ordered a corsage of pink roses for me and one of rosebuds for Lois Marie. I still have them among my souvenirs.)*

"We were shocked by the news of President Roosevelt's death. I wonder now how this will affect the history of the world. I did not vote for F.D.R. but I wish that he could have finished his term for he was much more of a leader than Truman is. I guess everything will be all right anyway.

"Last night I worked pretty late. We have a new daily report to turn in that is really a toughie. I sat on the bumper of my jeep with a typewriter on a box using the headlights of the jeep to write the report. Kinda makeshift, but it served the purpose."

* * * *

April 14, 1945: "I wished that you were here a few minutes ago to share the beautiful sunset with me. As the sun goes down the mountains change color from green to greenish blue, to blue, to purple, to violet, to dark gray, to dark. It was quite peaceful here, not much like the war that is all around us.

"Today I received four old issues of the L.S.A. bulletin. I see that Mrs. Lyle E. Young has renewed membership and that Lt. and Mrs. Young have contributed toward the new center."

* * * *

April 15-16, 1945: "We can now tell places we have been prior to our present location. They are in order; Townsville, Australia; Port Moresby, Dobadura or Ora Bay near Buna, Finschhaven, Aitape, Wakde (all on or near New Guinea), Morotai, Leyte, and our present (censored) location. The roughest, toughest of them all was Wakde. That little island was fortified heavily and the ground fighting was rough. Its size one mile by one-half mile made it a perfect bombing target, its white coral shining in the moonlight. I saw more death there than I'll ever see again. Someday I will tell you the whole story."

* * * *

April 18, 1945: "The changes in work since my promotion are few. A little more is expected of me now, but in turn I can expect a little more from others. The change is definitely a good one. Tonight we had shots for the plague. That is a new one we haven't had before.

"Do you remember how broke we were in Florida and Georgia? When we first got to Venice we had just come from home, had to pay insurance, hotels, etc., until we were in bad shape. Then in Waycross we had to wait until we got my lost pay check straightened out. We had some trying times there, but we got along happily." *(I don't remember any of that.)*

* * * *

April 19, 1945: "It has been several days since I've received a letter from you. I feel terribly lonely tonight. It is one of those moments when I am aware of the thousands of miles that are between us ... we shouldn't let the number of miles bother us. In reality it isn't any worse than one or two miles as long as we have to be apart. These thousands of miles can be quickly behind us when the opportunity comes. May that be soon."

* * * *

April 21, 1945: "Thank you for getting all the insignia. I've received one pair of Captain's bars and a pair of wings so far. I never realized how bright insignia are. Over here most insignia are rusted, corroded, very worn and dull.

"What a day. It is Sunday and theoretically a day off. I've had a mess of phone calls, an inspection, and this afternoon we had to load and ship out twelve aircraft engines. Each engine weighs a ton and a quarter so that is no easy job. Four of my men who were also supposed to have the day off stood by all day to help with the jobs. I can always depend on these men to work extra hours without a kick. It is wonderful to have such good cooperation from the men.

"I did get an hour this afternoon to visit Glenn after his appendix operation. He's getting along swell. Tomorrow I'm going to bring him some things he wants. It isn't pleasant to go to a hospital over here and see men suffering from different kinds of wounds. War is a horrible thing."

* * * *

April 24, 1945: "Tonight there was a lecture to give on Chemical Warfare. A certain amount of training must always be given. I sorta wish I'd never gone to that school in Venice. Ever since then I've had the extra duty of 'Gas Officer'. We are again doing the work of three Squadrons. It is the penalty we pay for having a good record."

* * * *

April 27, 1945: "Tomorrow I'm off to the big city. I have a pass and am in charge of twenty men going to Manila for two days, so will not be able to get completely away from responsibility."

* * * *

April 30, 1945: "About the trip to Manila. We left here Saturday morning in a B-17 and flew to Manila. After arriving we hitchhiked into the center of the city and spent the morning looking around. By 'we' I mean two Lts. and me. The prices are very high. A meal equivalent to a State side blue plate special for twenty-five cents cost about five pesos ($2.50). Found the home of my friend Jake Romero, but he had moved. The people there invited us in, nevertheless, in true Philippine hospitality. One of the Lts. had a friend in Manila that attended Notre Dame with him and he asked these people if they knew him. By coincidence they did. We then went to the home of this man's cousin who in turn invited us in for a drink and then directed us to the home of the Lts.' friend. That friend was from then on sort of a guide for us, and took us to a night club.

"The next morning we shopped, buying a few souvenirs for you at home. The city is in ruins. It is sorrowful to see the fine buildings and homes demolished. Most of the people we met were Spanish. They were the cream of society and treated us royally wherever we went. They lived a luxurious life before the war with many servants, cars and beautiful homes."

* * * *

May 3, 1945: "Today we heard of the death of Hitler and some of his henchmen. It looks like the war in Germany will peter out with no formal surrender. There are already steps being made to send men and equipment to this theater. I changed some of the men's jobs today. It is part of a program to have each man learn as many jobs as possible. I've now got quite a few men who can handle practically any job that comes up. The men like a change once in awhile too.

Whenever a man comes to me and wants a different job I've managed to find one for him. I guess my methods are a bit unorthodox, but they seem to work out swell and are popular with the men."

* * * *

May 5, 1945: "Glenn and I have been having quite a time fixing up our shack. It looked like rain so we decided to put up some side curtains. Last time it rained everything we owned got soaked. We had just started when the rain began to pour. We took off all our clothes and finished our work in the nude. Then we discovered holes in the roof so I got on top and with a can of tar in one hand and a piece of cloth in my mouth I patched holes with my free hand. When I finished I was tar all over so had to get some gasoline to get it off.

"We heard tonight that all Germans in Northern Germany and Denmark had surrendered … soon we shall see what our chances are of an early reunion. I think they are good for next fall. I can imagine the thrill of seeing our little daughter and all her cute little activities. Soon I can share the happiness of being a real parent to her."

* * * *

May 7, 1945: "Yesterday three of my men and I took my jeep and drove way back into the mountains. The road was little more than a path, but the rough ride was worth the experience. The mountains are very beautiful. The rocky hills rise abruptly from the winding ribbon of a river. Along their banks are many kinds of trees giving off shadows that were weird yet nice. All of us were married men and we kept remarking how swell it would be if the wives could see the scenery too.

"On the way back we stopped at a hut where a family of primitive people live, much like the New Guinea natives. They were very dirty and most of them diseased. They hunt with bows and arrows to get their food. Just before we got back we stopped to trade for some chickens. We had forgotten about dinner and knowing what Sunday suppers are like decided to make a real feast for ourselves. We cleaned the chickens, got some lard and flour from the mess hall to Southern fry them. One of the boys made some cocoa with condensed milk and chocolate. A couple of other fellows joined us and the six of us ate six chickens. Boy, what a treat that was. Gosh, I wish you could have been there for the sightseeing tour and chicken fry.

"In a few days I may go to the hospital to have my cyst removed. *The cyst was at the base of his spine.* It is a simple operation but will take quite a while to heal completely. I think it is a good time to get it done before I am eligible for rotation."

* * * *

May 8, 1945: "Today is V-E day. Everyone here is surprisingly calm. Few of the men mentioned it. It means little to us now until they start pouring in from Europe. I imagine people in the States celebrated in a big way. I hope they don't forget us over here. We still have a big job to do. I wonder what Japan will do now.

"The Doc was just in before leaving for his date with a nurse. I think this affair must be getting serious because he sees her every night. This is the only romance I've seen since being overseas. Some of the officers and men have dates with nurses, WACs and Red Cross girls when they are around. The proportion of men to women is about 500 to one so you can see what competition the single men have. We hear that in the States the man shortage is pretty bad. Do the girls whistle at the boys?"

* * * *

May 11, 1945: "Today came three wonderful letters to cheer me. I went over to the hospital and had the surgeon examine my cyst. Monday morning will have the operation. He said it would take quite a while to heal as the opening cannot be stitched. It has to heal from the inside out, and that my hospitalization period will be from two to five weeks. The hospital is quite close to the Squadron so it will be easy to have mail delivered."

* * * *

May 13, 1945: "Today I had to make a special report to the colonel. The officer who is to take my place while I'm in the hospital came, and I showed him around and gave him a few instructions. This new officer just landed from the States on May 1st. He says there are a lot of men on the way over. Tomorrow I go to the hospital. If I don't write for a few days, don't worry. The operation is a simple one."

* * * *

May 15, 1945: "I haven't had my operation yet. So far all the attention I've had is the taking of a blood count. This is quite a large hospital. The wards are big long tents with two rows of cots in them. Each ward has its own ward man and nurse. Even now they have a lot of patients, so we seldom see them."

* * * *

May 17, 1945: "Lying here with little I can do there is no better way to pass the time than think of my girls at home. I have your pictures beside me as a special kind of inspiration. They said that I asked for your picture first thing when I came out of anesthesia. Next to the weather it is said that people most often talk about their operation. Well, it happened Wed. morning. I was given a shot of morphine and then walked to the surgery tent. They shot some sodium pentothal into a vein in my arm and told me to start counting. I got to about eight and don't remember another thing. I woke up a few hours later with a bandage as big as a house on my wound. Since then I've felt ok but find it very uncomfortable to lay on my side and stomach only. I get a shot of penicillin every two hours. I've had about 25 now and still have a bunch to take. Both arms feel like a pincushion."

* * * *

May 19, 1945: "How is the little princess? If I don't mention Lois Marie very often it isn't because I don't think of her. It is that I don't know what to say. I have her pictures and your letters to tell me the highlights of her activities. All this I treasure, but it is such a small part of what knowing and seeing her would be. I know that she is a charming, lovable little girl, but we are still strangers. I pray that it won't be for much longer.

"I finished my shots of penicillin this morning. In all there were 36 of them so it was quite an ordeal. The doctor also let me get up and walk a little. I found that I wasn't as sturdy as I thought I was going to be. Consequently, I've been in bed most of the day. Just the same it's nice to get up and stand once in awhile. Course, I can't sit with my sitter in tremendous bandages. Fred Herman and a Sgt. dropped in for a visit. I've had plenty of visitors. The Sgt. gave me a half pack of cigarettes which sure were welcome.

"I got morale to spare today, five of your wonderful letters. About the pictures: the Squadron picture was grouped by flights. This grouping is purely for tactical use, defense, etc., so it isn't used often. The gremlin with the wrench is our insignia. The pictures of planes are all B-24s (Liberator Bombers). The ant hills are those that dot the landscape of Northern Australia. They are made of mud carried by ants and are as hard as concrete."

* * * *

May 21, 1945: "Today I had a heat lamp treatment to enhance healing conditions, the Doc says." *In the hospital Lyle read many books, did a lot of dreaming about what life will be like when he is home and we have a home of our own.* "Lois Marie was there to 'help' and ask questions: 'Daddy, when you gonna shave? I wanna see you make funny faces when you do'." *He dreamed on,* "We fixed a picnic lunch and drove into the country, found a nice grassy, shady place and spread out a blanket. Then we went on a little exploration tour. Lois Marie walked along quietly for awhile and then toddled ahead to pick a flower or examine a bug. We walked arm in arm enjoying the closeness of each other and watching the little princess. Soon we'd go back and build a fire to cook wieners. Lois Marie asked why Daddy blew on the fire and might even help …"

* * * *

May 24, 1945: "This life in the hospital is getting pretty tiresome. I'm healing in good shape cuz I feel as good as ever. I have to take a half hour under the heat lamp which on a hot day doesn't help any. The perspiration pours out of me. They keep my bandage wet with glycerin all the time. I was permitted to go to the mess hall for my meals, no more breakfast in bed. Hope I can get out pretty soon."

* * * *

May 25, 1945: "Another of those month overseas anniversaries, 22 months. Anyway we have that much time behind us. Last night a traveling GI show put on a program. I haven't laughed like that for so long. There were plenty of jokes, skits, tricks and music. With an all male audience there wasn't much care taken to keep the show clean, but it wasn't too bad to be good entertainment. There was a mouth organist, tenor, and accordion players to furnish a lot of music. Everyone thought the show was swell."

* * * *

May 26, 1945: "Not much happened at the hospital today. I had an X-ray taken of my thumb that I crushed awhile back. The thumb doesn't seem to be healing fast enough. I've lost the nail and hope a new one grows back ok. I can look out of the tent and see planes coming back from a mission. They fly in formation until over the strip and then peal off one at a time and get in a single line which circles the strip before landing. Soon we should see vast clouds of planes instead of our little trickle. I've yet to see a B-29. Sure would like to see one. They've been doing a big job on the Nip islands.

"Had a few visitors today. The men have been very busy and are wondering when I'm coming back. I hope it's soon. Today the radio brings news of Tokyo still burning from the last B-29 raids. High winds are driving the fires. The fire bombs that we are using are very effective. The back of my lap has lost its soreness, and I feel fit as a fiddle again. Doc says I'll have to stay awhile yet until I'm all healed up.

"There is a rifle, machine gun, mortar, and grenade range right near here and there is a heck of a racket most of the day. They picked a good spot near a hospital quiet zone. I don't particularly mind it, however, for I'm used to a lot of racket near an airstrip where planes are always warming up and buzzing around. M/Sgt. McAfee, my chief man was just here to see me. He says everything is going ok, but they are really busy. No one can say that our outfit hasn't done more than its share since we've been here. Never have we been so busy over such a long stretch of months. Things never seem to let up. Nothing like keeping busy though. I sure find that out in the hospital with little to do."

* * * *

June 1, 1945: "I got out of the hospital for a few minutes this afternoon on a pass. I called the Squadron and they sent a jeep over after me. I spent most of the afternoon down on the line inspecting things and talking to the men. I'll be glad when I can go back and stay ... The highlight of the day was five letters from you ... Today everyone started driving on the right side of the road. The old business of driving on the left, a hangover from Australia, is gone forever. It is like learning to drive all over again."

* * * *

June 5, 1945: "It's awfully quiet around here. There aren't as many patients now. Hope there is one less real soon. The Doc doesn't give me much satisfaction as to when I can get out. He says, 'It won't be long'. When I get out I'll have to be careful for a month or so, not able to lift much weight or ride in a jeep. That won't stop me from doing my work because I can walk to work."

* * * *

June 6, 1945: "Today marks one year since the invasion of France. They cleaned that up in less than a year. I wonder how much longer it will take here."

* * * *

June 7, 1945: "The doctor said yesterday that I'd have to stay in the hospital another week. The incision isn't quite healed yet. There is no soreness or pain so it is hard to be inactive while feeling so spry. I'm still getting daily heat lamp treatments and otherwise I'm free of attention."

* * * *

June 9, 1945: "The Squadron called yesterday morning and wanted me to get out on a pass. Some business came up concerning personnel. I arranged the pass ok. At the Squadron I spent the rest of the day settling that problem. Got up to date on everything that's going on and switched some men around to other jobs. This was necessary because they took one of my key men away to make him a 1st Sgt. In the evening the men had a surprise pork barbeque and chicken fry in my honor. They were expecting me out of the hospital for good. My pass was only good until 6:00, but with the party I couldn't very well leave, so I overstayed my pass. The men had bought a small pig and six chickens. They placed them on a spit and had been turning and basting them over the hot coals all day. It was delicious. We had bread to make sandwiches. I thought that was darn nice of the fellows. Glad they think I'm ok.

"In your letter of May 25th you and Lois Marie were having a pretty fair time in Granite. Mom had a few neighbors in. I know that you enjoy the company of older women as much as younger people, but Judy Sween was there who is just a little older than we." *(I always enjoyed Lyle's mother and her friends ... never thought about age.)*

* * * *

June 11, 1945: "The Nip government announced on the radio today, 'The American bombing of Japan is unfair. It is disrupting the life of the Japanese people'. Their propaganda is the crudest possible and serves only to amuse the American soldier.

"I have quite a bit of accrued leave time to collect when I go on inactive status. A soldier is allowed 30 days leave a year and if it isn't taken he is paid his regular pay. I will have something like 70 days coming. By the way I have a 3-year hitch in today. Now I get $10.00 more a month. We didn't think three years ago as I left on that bus from Monte that this would take so long."

* * * *

June 13, 1945: 'It is good to be out of the hospital and back at my table to write to you. I came out this morning and Glenn went in this afternoon. He has been suffering from severe headaches and the doctors found the muscles in his eyes were weak. He will be gone a week to ten days in which time he'll exercise his eyes, relax, etc., under hospital supervision."

* * * *

June 16, 1945: "I am Commanding Officer of the Squadron for a few days while the Major is away. This in addition to my other duties, so I'm swamped. Being C.O. it was my job to host our Group Commander, Col. Powell and his Red Cross girlfriend. I met them as they drove up, saluted, and escorted them to their reserved seats for the stage show from Manila. Throughout the show I had to think up polite remarks and answers on several numbers. Afterwards we went to the mess hall for coffee and some ice cream made in our ice box. Then a salute and 'Good night, Sir, Good night, Miss', and my duties as a host were over."

* * * *

June 19-20, 1945: "It rained all last night and all morning. The little creek near our area overrun its banks and almost washed away between our living and working areas. The rain here is in even greater quantity than in New Guinea, but the rolling terrain is better suited to drainage, so it isn't as disagreeable. The men who are coming here now think this is terrible, but they are lucky not to have to put up with the jungle, reptiles and utter wildness. Then, too, the living conditions, food, entertainment, mail service, equipment and roads are all so much better here. We are finally getting supplies here.

"The army is sure changing overseas. Regulations on correct uniforms and military courtesy are coming out right and left. Once was when we had only to worry about doing our job. Now we have to watch our dress, our men's dress, and all that sort of thing. It distracts a lot from our work and all this 'spit and polish' will only prolong the war. There is too much work to be done and a war to be won.

"This afternoon we had a lot of supplies to ship. It poured all afternoon so we worked in the rain and the mud. I took my shirt off and pitched in too. You should have seen us when we finished, mud from head to toe and soaked. We got five trucks loaded and shipped out which isn't bad for an afternoon.

"Thanks for the financial statement. I've never in my life had over a couple hundred dollars at my disposal and now we have almost three and a half thousand. You are doing swell, honey. I'm proud of you. Yes, I think we should have charge accounts with the butcher, baker, etc., and pay at the end of each month. It is very convenient that way."

* * * *

June 25, 1945: "It was two long years ago that we were last together. We have two years of our time behind us. This being apart is like a prison sentence put on us by a world at war. Today I found that I'm authorized to wear another campaign star so that brings my points up to 84. Today is also 23 months overseas. Slowly I'm compiling enough time and points to give me a higher priority toward the day I start home.

"Glenn is back from the hospital. We have been gabbing so much that we have hardly found time to write. It is good to have his company again during the evenings. We have been indulging to the extent of three cans of beer and a cigar. The talk has drifted from rotation and the point system to politics international, then business, accounting and almost everything. I hope that Glenn and Joyce will decide to make Minnesota their home cuz we could get together for some good times.

"Jeanette *(a cousin)* and Fred must have had a very nice wedding. As you say, there is a certain glamour in a big wedding. I'd have liked to see you in your blue gown as the lovely bride's matron.

"I've got a miserably sore throat tonight. Everyone has had colds and now it must be my turn. We are all so run down from two years of vitamin deficiency and other things lacking in our food that we are subject to all kinds of disorders. Lt. Casey, the pilot I told you about from Mpls., is in the hospital now. He has a bad case of amoebic dysentery. I was over to see him this afternoon and found him improving. There is more darn sickness around here.

"Everyone is very angry with all those strikes in the States. These men are earning several times as much as they would in the army. They are with their families and friends. There is no danger. Yet they lay down on the job making it harder for the men over here. I think that for the rest of my life I'll be against any kind of union. I'd like to see the government draft each striker and send them over here to replace a man that would give almost anything to trade places."

Lyle wrote of all the shows (movies) that came to the men. He seems to have seen hundreds of movies and to have read many, many books in these years of limited recreation.

* * * *

July 9, 1945: "Three came today, your inspiring letters of June 26, 27, and 28. Thank you for boosting the ol' morale like that. Your letters are so important to me. We had a busy day today. During the rainy season we must 'make hay while the sun shines'. We've had three or four nice days in a row, but it's raining again. A good part of our work is receiving aircraft parts and supplies and shipping parts that are damaged to depts. to repair. The Squadron is able to do a lot of repair work here, but we haven't the equipment or personnel for bigger work. For the last few days we've been receiving and shipping a lot of supplies via air transport. We hear of carrier-based planes bombing the Tokyo area without opposition. Admiral Halsey challenged the Nip navy to come out and fight. Also 600 B-29s, Iwo based P-51s and B-24s and B-25s of the Fifth Air Force hit Japan. If bombing alone could defeat the Nips we'd be getting there fast. I'm afraid that it will take a lot of slugging by the infantry before the victory.

"Heard from Bud today *(Lyle's brother.)* He's very interested in his surveying job. I'd like to see him go into Civil Engineering if he has a liking for mathematics. I got quite a kick out of him talking about taking levels, figuring out ton miles of dirt and plotting profiles. He's on his way."

* * * *

July 14, 1945: "Today the first man from our organization got his orders to go home. He has 104 points. The fleet of Admiral Halsey is still pestering the Nips more than somewhat. I guess he's working on his project 'If Japan goes on fighting we'll bomb them until the islands will be nothing more than a menace to aviation'. The B-29s are putting about 500 planes daily over Japan and medium bombers and fighters are doing their part. I hope this effort results in more than impressing the Nips."

* * * *

July 15-16, 1945: "Another exceptionally busy day. I had to use all my men for these two days in spite of the fact they were supposed to have a day off. They have worked in the rain most of the time. I've been soaked myself for two days, except in the evenings. Raincoats are of little help in these downpours. It soaks right through them in a few minutes. Being wet isn't bad when one gets used to it. It's warm enough.

"I'm glad you received the souvenirs ok. Thanks for setting me straight that those 'woven table mats' were needlepoint pieces for pillow tops. *I forgot about the needlepoint until the early 1980s when I bought yarn at Miller & Paine and finished them.*
"Yes, I think it would be nice to own a really good painting as the basis for doing a

living room." *We bought an original water color of Colorado's Meeker Mountain and Longs Peak in 1990 ... sometimes dreams take a few years to materialize.*

* * * *

July 25, 1945: "I can't think of a definite wedding gift for Jean and Ervin. Let's give them $50.00 to use as they like. When Gordon and Eunice get married we can give them the same gift." *(Both couples were married before Lyle came home.)*

"These last two days have been exceptionally busy. It's not over yet for the next few will be the same. Right in the middle of the muddle a letter from you came. Darling, I wish I could tell you how much that meant to me."

Okinawa, Japan 1945

On a ship to Okinawa in July 1945

Captain Lyle Young — Cabin mate Lieutenant Glenn Bowerman

Landing Ship Tank (L.S.T.) landing at Okinawa 1945

Japanese envoys arriving at Ie Shima. First physical contact after war's end. August 19, 1945. Lyle was not on Ie Shima, but that island is very close to Okinawa and they could see the planes.

The C-54 Americans used to carry Japanese to the Battleship Missouri where the Japanese surrender papers were signed, ending the war in the Pacific

August 4, 1945: "I am on a ship anchored in a harbor on Luzon. We've been here for two days now taking on fuel, water, and supplies. This is our third day aboard. Tearing down our installations, packing and loading it all aboard was the same tremendous job it always is. I worked right through two whole days and the night between. When it was all done I was sweaty, dirty with beard, and very, very tired. We finished loading about 5 p.m. so right after chow I took a bath and went to bed. I'm my old sassy self again." *(He was on the way to Okinawa.)*

"As usual during these trips we are enjoying the Navy's luxuries of sheets and food served in the civilian way. Our duties aboard are very few so we just lounge around, talk and read. Yesterday some of the ship's officers took all of our officers ashore in a small boat to the Navy Officer's Club. Like all navy installations, it was very nice. They served cold beer and drinks. The navy men aboard got their first mail in 60 days yesterday. They can have all their superior living conditions. I'll take our mail service."

* * * *

August 10, 1945: "We are still at sea. The letter I wrote a few days ago is still here. Couldn't get it mailed before so you will probably get that one with this. For two days we went through a storm. The ship rocked and rolled until I thought it would roll completely over. A guy didn't know whether to walk on the floor or the walls, both were equally level. We had to chain down all our vehicles to the deck to keep them from going overboard. Most of us were seasick throughout the two days. I didn't feel so bad as long as I stayed in my bunk. Navy bunks are rather like a box to keep from falling out in bad weather. It is rather uncomfortable bouncing off the sides of the box for hours at a time.

"When the storm let up we had a little game of tag with a couple of Nip submarines, which we won. We heard this morning about Russia's declaration of war against Japan and our new weapon, the atomic bomb. This atomic bomb sounds like something out of Buck Rogers and has great potential."

Their first reports of the atomic bomb said that a new bomb equal to 10,000 tons of TNT had the zeros crossed out (like zeros with slashes through them), and the men thought it much less. Only later did they learn the actual power of the atomic bombs.

* * * *

August 14, 1945: Somewhere in the Western Pacific. "Well, darling, we have finally arrived at our destination so that I can mail this letter. It has been a full two weeks in which I haven't been able to mail a single letter. I put in another of those day and night work marathons and now your hubby is very tired."

* * * *

The hard-fought battles by the navy and army to win Okinawa were actions to make possible the invasion of Japan. Thousands of men in our army and navy were lost, the most in any previous naval campaign. And yet Japan lost tens of thousands of soldiers and even more civilians. That victory was achieved on June 21, 1945. American B-29s continued to bomb Japan in hopes of making them surrender, but they would not given in.

In order to finally win in the Pacific, the United States decided to drop an atomic bomb on Hiroshima on August 6, 1945. Still the Japanese did not surrender, so the U.S. felt is necessary to drop the second bomb, this time on Nagasaki on August 9th. The Russians declared war on Manchuria, and on August 15, 1945, Japan surrendered.

* * * *

August 15, 1945: A.P.O. 37, Okinawa. "Tonight there is peace on earth. The bloody beaches, screaming bombs and fear is gone. Now we must be patient with the reconstruction. The news was taken calmly here. We have too much work to be done to make our area livable, so no one has time for celebration. The men went about their work without any apparent show of feeling. The 1st Sgt. had to get after three or four that thought they'd loaf now that the peace had come.

"There are two reasons why the news was received so indifferently. First the men know our life will be little changed for some months and they are saving the celebration for when they go home. Second, the final results after four or five days of consideration was an anticlimax to the original announcement by the Nips that they wanted to quit. It is too early yet to know just how I will stand toward getting home, but it will be much sooner than if the war were going on. Don't be too optimistic, honey, for the army has a tremendous job of demobilizing the Nips, occupying Japan, and then sending millions of tons of equipment and a couple million of men home. I will tell you all that I can find out as soon as the news becomes available. Let's keep our fingers crossed, huh? Anyway, now we know that I will get home definitely.

"Today I've had a detail of men working on a shower and laundry for the Squadron. We should have it all in full operation by tomorrow evening. We have a temporary shower now made with just an eight foot length of pipe with small holes in it. With 230 men one doesn't get much of a bath, but we must have something for it is very hot and everyone sweats a lot. It is just about dark so I will tell you something about Okinawa tomorrow."

* * * *

August 16, 1945: "Okinawa is a beautiful island. The terrain is rolling and rocky and covered with vegetation throughout. It is semi-tropical. There are few large trees, but lots of hedges and bushes. The island has a large population which was once non-Nipponese, but now after long Jap rule the people can be practically considered Japanese. Now the army has all civilians restricted to certain areas to keep them from interfering with operations. The main occupation of the people was farming although an American wouldn't even attempt to farm this land. The soil is red clay. There is still a great deal of coral rock on the surface which natives remove by hand and dispose of by building fences. These fences wander everywhere dividing the one or two acre farms into little patches. No piece of ground is too small to plant some kind of crop. The steep hillsides are terraced to give a little more space.

"The farm buildings are small huts squeezed into a little space. The buildings have stone walls and thatched roofs. They are rather neatly fitted into little clumps of trees and bushes with stone walls all around. I have wandered through a lot of these farms for our area is situated in the middle of some of them. I have picked up a few souvenirs which might be interesting.

"Another interesting thing on the island is their method of burial. Everywhere are concrete monuments to the dead of the family. The custom of ancestor worship is in great evidence. Often these monuments are more elaborate and expensive than the houses they live in. The monuments consist of a vault in which the bones are laid after cremation and around which is fancy oriental ornamentation.

"The Okinawan women are very oriental looking with dark eyes, olive skin, and straight black hair. All are very short and plump. They dress in a blouse and form of bloomers that fit very tightly at the waist and ankles. They are all very cheerful and often sing those weird Nip songs at work. They are very industrious. Here is a 10 yen note of military currency to add to the collection. One yen equals a dime, so this note is only worth a dollar. Yes, we are being paid with this stuff now."

* * * *

August 19, 1945: "Today I was witness to an important bit of history. I saw the Nip diplomats arrive in their two white planes on Ie Shima and leave in one of our C-54s. It even was broadcast in the States so you might have heard the commentary on it. This is the first contact with the Nips personally since the beginning of the end. About now the Nips should be landing in Manila. So far the surrender seems to be progressing slowly, but satisfactorily. We've had doubts of their sincerity but they are sticking to the terms so far. It will be a big job to take care of disarming and occupying Japan. I don't know just what part we will play in that task.

"The bulk of our Squadron celebrated two years of overseas service last night. We had a Tarzan show, then beer and hamburgers at the mess hall. The highlight of the evening was fresh onions which we had with our burgers. I was never particularly fond of onions, but after a time without them a person develops unexplainable desires for such foods. Still no mail. I hope it catches up soon.

"I have a lecture to give to the Squadron on the Japanese people and Japan. I've been reading all available literature on the Nip people, their character, beliefs, philosophy, way of life, etc. I am getting to the point where I understand the 'why' for a lot of the Nip's unnatural actions and beliefs.

"The men have a new hitch to the 'Dear John' clubs. (Letters from jilting wives and girlfriends always begin with 'Dear John'.) Now when a man finds that a girl or wife has found someone else he hangs her picture on the wall of the latrine with a sign like 'She found a sugar daddy' or 'She married a U.S.O. Commando'. I'll admit that this is pretty crude humor, but the pet hate of men over here is unfaithful women.

"Chalk up another month to the ol' man's credit. This makes 25 away from the good old USA and 26 away from you. Sometimes, honey, I don't know how we've taken all this separation. Today orders came through to send all enlisted men with 85 points or more home by October lst. Officers are still as uncertain as ever. It will be another big day when I hit Frisco. You will know of that with letter, telegram, and telephone, if possible. Starting next Monday we are going to be soldiers again wearing full uniform, with all shoulder patches, insignia, shoes must be shined, and saluting and 'sirs' will be the rule. It looks like I am going to have to do a bit of sewing tomorrow to get all my uniforms in order. I guess this is intended to impress the Japanese that we have good discipline and military bearing."

* * * *

August 29, 1945: "This noon we took a Squadron picture for some official record. I wish there was some way to get a copy. This afternoon I took the PX inventory and made up my report to take to the main office tomorrow morning. I dread the long dirty ride. We have had the first of a series of encephalitis shots: encephalitis is supposed to be common in Japan. I'm sending you a bunch of pictures taken at our last station. We sure hated to leave it as it was the best camp we ever had. Glenn took these and Joyce had reprints made."

* * * *

September 2, 1945: "I'm blue and worried. Tonight I received a telegram from Dad telling me that Mom is to have an operation on the sixth. I've been trying all day to get an emergency furlough, but I've had to give up. I was told that it was necessary to have an investigation by the Red Cross at home as to the urgency of my being at home. The Red Cross director said that would take three weeks. Other avenues proved hopeless also. I feel helpless over here. All I can do is pray everything will be all right. I told Dad we'd help with expenses so that Mom could have the best care possible."

* * * *

September 5, 1945: "All censorship is over. I can tell you where we are. We are located just across from Ie Shima on Okinawa. Our set up is only temporary for we are supposed to move into Japan before long. We expect to be near Shimonoseki or Yawata on Southern Kyushu. I imagine we'll go up by boat in a couple of weeks … Got paid today, 2518 yen. Sounds like a fortune, but it is $167.85. The yen has dropped to $.06667 now so it takes a bale of the stuff to amount to much.

"Honey, will you send by first class air mail all the papers I sent to you from Waycross. I might have need for some of these records."

* * * *

September 6, 1945: "Today is the day Mom is to have her operation. I've been a bit worried all day,. There is still no more word from Dad since the telegram four days ago. I hope I get mail from Dad or you tomorrow to boost my morale."

* * * *

September 8, 1945: "Your wonderful letter today brought me out of the blues and cheered me about Mom's operation, and that all preparations for transfusions are being made. Still don't know what the operation is for."

* * * *

September 10, 1945: "I may be jumping the gun, but it might be time for you to send my winter uniforms to Mr. Arnold Anfinson, 123 Serrano Drive, Park Merced, in San Francisco, California. If I get home in the next couple of months I'll need these things for I'll be very thin blooded after all these months of heat. I have written to Arnie. Send it parcel post and insure the package for about $130.00.

"Dad's letter came today gave me the details of Mom's trouble. It sounds very serious. I know it is my duty to be there but I just can't manage to get an emergency leave."

* * * *

September 14, 1945: "The plan I told you about is official. With my 86 points I'm eligible to return to the U.S. in 60 days from Sept. 2nd. Now if everything goes ok I'll soon be able to write 'I'm coming home'. Then after two or three weeks of waiting we'll be able to talk to each other over the telephone. Then in another week or so we'll meet never to part like this again. At that moment we will begin a new and happy life.

"I'm glad Jean and Ervin's wedding was so nice, and I'm happy Gordon and Eunice have set the date for their wedding. Soon it will be our anniversary again, and I'm sorry to miss that again. Our third anniversary. Happy anniversary, darling.

"Today I received a telegram from Dad that Mom's condition is very critical. It was sent 9 days ago. Dad said that the Red Cross telegram was on its way. However, after applying it will take a week or two to go up the ladder to the highest headquarters for approval and then back down again. As for flying home it will depend on whether planes are available from the occupation of Japan by the time my orders come through. There is a possibility my chance to go home on redeployment will come about as fast as the emergency leave. I pray to God that Mom will be all right."

* * * *

September 18, 1945: "I have two swell letters from you. I needed their inspiration these last two days. We have just gone through a peachy hurricane. The wind started up Sunday morning. We worked hard trying to keep the tent up all day and night until 4 a.m. when our tent ripped to pieces. We fared better than most for our tent was one of the last to go down. With all this wind we had a steady downpour of rain which soaked everything. By yesterday morning every tent and the mess hall were flat.

"All our clothes and belongings were wet and muddy. Glenn lost all his clothes. They blew away. Our stuff was scattered all over the countryside. I fared exceptionally well cuz I had all my belongings packed so they stayed pretty much together. Yesterday the wind went down some and the rain let up so we slept last night in trucks and under ponchos. The storm was gone this morning. Glenn and I set up a little 6 x 9 tent in a very sheltered place and are quite comfortable now. We were fortunate having no one badly injured with flying debris.

"We seem to be set back on our move to Japan. We are the only Service Squadron left to take care of a bunch of tactical Squadrons, so I suppose that is why we are held here. I'd like to see Japan but the headaches and work involved aren't worth it unless I were to be there quite awhile, and I don't want that. I wanna go home."

* * * *

September 21, 1945: "My heart is heavy tonight. Today's mail brought your letters with the sad news about Mother. It was and is a shock even though I should have half expected it. If only the Red Cross verification would come through I could try for an emergency leave again. Today I tried to get a high priority of redeployment, but even though I'm eligible they will give me no help. If I can get an emergency leave I think I can stay in the States for over there they pay some attention to points. I simply must get home some way. It is our duty now to keep Mom as happy as possible and to help Dad too. It will be hard to be cheerful when inside one is sad, but we must do it somehow. I know that Dad will take it especially hard and my heart aches for him too.

"I have concluded that the best course of action to follow is to live as if no emergency existed. I think it would be easier for Mom and all of us to do that. Remember the weeks in Waycross when we knew we would be parted soon. We would not let ourselves talk or think much about it. Up until the last couple of days we were successful in keeping our spirits high. I think the same sort of logic will hold now.

"Darling, I think it might be safe for you not to write any more letters. If this should fall through I'll tell you to start writing again. I will continue to write until the news is definite and I will call you from Frisco or wherever I land in the U.S. I hope it is Frisco for my uniforms should be there. Yes?

"From Hawley, Minnesota I got a letter saying that Arnie Anfinson had been transferred to Seattle. Mrs. August Anfinson, Arnie's mother, suggested that I send Lyle's clothes to Arnie's aunt and uncle, Dr. and Mrs. Jim Anderson, in Petaluma, California, only 40 miles from Frisco. Petaluma is easily reached by bus. Lyle should call them and make sure the clothes have arrived."

* * * *

September 26, 1945: A.P.O. 337, Casual Detachment. "Tonight I'm on Ie Shima. Five officers and I who have known each other and worked together for all our overseas time are living in a tent together. We left our area early this morning and came over here by boat. We set up our tent and now have nothing to do but wait for the boat that will take us to Frisco. We are now in the 321st Squadron of the 90th Bomb Group (The Jolly Rodgers). We may either go back as a complete unit or as individuals. I have no idea how long I'll be here, but things don't look too promising. It may be a couple of weeks. I would like you to meet me in Minneapolis when I return as we planned. I'll telegraph or call you."

* * * *

September 27, 1945: "I saw a lot of old friends here today from outfits we've worked with throughout Australia, Guinea, Philippines and here. There are a big bunch of us waiting for our ship to come in."

* * * *

September 29, 1945: "Right now we are sweating out another typhoon. Weather reports say that the edge of it will hit here unless the wind changes a little. Hope so, for I'd hate to spend another night without a home."

* * * *

September 30, 1945: "Here we are still on Ie Shima. It seems we can't get the least bit of information as to when or how we're going home. It is the same old army way. Wait, wait, wait. Then all of a sudden we'll be rushed to get started. This lying around is getting darn tiresome. We visit a lot of old friends, but now that we've caught up on all the topics of conversation, it's very dull."

* * * *

October 4th, 1945: "We are just getting over another hurricane or typhoon. The wind has been blowing for three days and nights and with it we had a lot of rain. The wind is dying down now and the rain has stopped. These days have been miserable. We were able to keep our tent upright by almost constant mooring. But even then the rain came in the sides and got most of our stuff wet. It has been cold too, so that we could stay warm only by staying in bed and that wasn't entirely successful.

"We were supposed to go by boat to the southern tip of Okinawa a couple days ago, but the storm stopped all that. At this point we were to have our records checked and get orders to return to the States. Now we don't know how we stand.

"Did you get the flowers for our anniversary yesterday? This year we are closer to reunion than ever before, and now we are assured definitely that being apart for an anniversary will never happen again."

* * * *

October 6, 1945: "Yesterday 2000 of us loaded on a Landing Ship Tank at Ie Shima and came here to Yonton on the southern tip of Okinawa. We are now assigned to the 380th Bomb Group who will send us to the States. We have already turned in our records to be checked and they have the necessary information for cutting our orders. Everyone feels a little better. It gets cold here. I froze last night. It has been a couple weeks since I've had mail. I guess I'll not get any more mail, but will next speak to you from Frisco."

* * * *

October 8, 1945: "We are in another typhoon. This one is rather mild. It did rain a lot though, and our tent leaks so we are all pretty damp. What I'd give to get out of this part of the world. There are thousands of men here to take care of so that checking records and making duplicate orders for each man and loading on ships are all things that take days rather than just hours. I think that when we reach the States we will run into less delay for they are better equipped to handle us."

* * * *

October 12, 1945: "I'm sorry that I've failed to write in the last 4 days. We are just getting back to normal after another typhoon. This typhoon was the grand daddy of them all. The wind started Sunday night and blew fairly hard until Tuesday afternoon. We managed to keep our tent up until then, but at three o'clock it ripped all to pieces. The wind rose in velocity until 8 p.m. Tuesday when it blew at 150 miles per hour. I was out in the middle of it all. I stayed behind a sturdy tree to protect me from flying boards, oil drums, etc., hung on there all night. I was soaked to the skin and shook with the cold all night. Wednesday morning the wind went down a little and we managed to put up another tent and build a gasoline fire to keep warm. Yesterday it cleared up and we got most of our clothes dried out.

"This morning I washed out some clothes in a mud puddle; there is no water for anything but drinking. We've been eating emergency rations and probably will continue to do so for the mess hall blew away too. There were a few men killed, but for the most part it just made us homeless. That radio said 90,000 homeless, but that count was after most of us had a chance to set up again. These last few days, and especially Tuesday, were the most miserable moments I've ever spent."

* * * *

October 16, 1945: "You have given the old morale another boost. I managed to get two of your letters from the Squadron last night. One was a swell birthday card, timely as today I am 26. As far as I know we are only waiting for ships. That is ironical to me for we need only to go up on a hill near camp and see at least a hundred ships in the harbor. The army wasn't fussy about what accommodations we had on the way over, but for some reason they have only a few select ships on which they'll send men back. They don't realize that I'd shovel coal on a tramp steamer or anything else to get back.

"Your letters were written from Granite Falls. I was somewhat relieved that Mom was feeling somewhat well. You mention Meta. They are swell letters, and I conclude that Meta Schulz is at home. She is very capable and a swell girl. She knows the family and so is excellent for the job.

"I am glad you have sent my uniforms to Arnie, and the long handled underwear too. I shall need it, I think."

* * * *

October 18, 1945: "Two new letters from you today to read with all the others when I am lonely, and that's pretty often. The article in the Star Journal about the need for civil engineers looks good. Maybe I'll not have too much trouble finding a job. The sooner we settle down the sooner we'll have that home of our own. Seven hundred men left today and 1000 are leaving tomorrow. There must be 7000 here all waiting.

"Another small group of officers and men left this morning. I expect a large bunch to go out in the next few days and hope to be in it. Yesterday we got some fresh potatoes via the Navy and fixed up a grill out of a piece of iron. We had a wonderful feast. I didn't realize that real potatoes were so much better than dehydrated ones. We get two meals a day from the mess hall and manage to chisel enough stuff to make the dinner ourselves. Our own handiwork is usually superior cuz the mess hall is feeding a couple thousand men and they can take no pains in preparation (opening cans). Some of the boats leaving are going to Seattle. I hope I'm on one going to Frisco for I'll need my uniforms."

* * * *

October 26, 1945: "I just finished doing some laundry. When we left the outfit I intended throwing away clothes as they became dirty, but we are here longer than I expected so I had to wash some out. I always have dreaded washing clothes. I sympathize with women for that task. I guess a washing machine makes some difference.

"Our plight is discouraging. Only a few officers have left in the last few days. You can imagine how I feel when I see officers with as little as four months overseas leaving before I do. These men have more points than I do due to the unfair method of awarding campaign stars. When I inquire 'Why the delay?' I am told there are no ships available. Yet I can count about a hundred laying in the harbor. Many of these have been idle for weeks. No use trying to understand the army."

* * * *

November 3, 1945: "I had hoped to be home for a celebration of Lois Marie's second birthday and then Thanksgiving, but now I can only hope for Christmas."

* * * *

November 6, 1945: "A big two stacker troop ship came into the harbor yesterday causing no end of rumors and speculation. I hope it is used here and not sent somewhere else. Even if it doesn't take me it will take a lot of men ahead of me putting me higher on the rotation list. I just got back from chow. I talked with a Captain who gave me awful news. The system of sending Fifth Air Force officers home as individuals has been stopped at 90 points and all of them will be sent home with units. There is no telling when I'll get home now. Maybe you'd better start writing again. All I can say is that some of these days it will all work out."

* * * *

November 9, 1945: "If I were home today we'd have a nice big cake with two candles on it to match the sparkle in Lois Marie's eyes. Yesterday I moved again. We are still with the 380th Bomb Group but living in a different spot. The Red Cross verification of Mom's illness came through finally, so I put in for immediate return to the States. The Adjutant here tells me that a lot of other men have put in similar applications and have been turned down, so??? Anything is worth a try."

* * * *

November 12, 1945: "Yesterday I moved again. Now I'm living just a few feet from the tent I had in the 380th Casual Detachment, yet now I'm under the 312th Bomb Group. Most of the men leaving here go to Seattle or L.A,. or some port other than Frisco. This messes up getting my uniforms from Arnie. So I wrote him today and had him send them to Betty in St. Paul. That way no matter where I land I'll have an equal chance of getting them. I can manage across the country ok for I will be probably on a troop train any way."

* * * *

This was Lyle's last letter from overseas. Surprisingly, I'd never opened the envelope. On the morning of January 17, 1995 (more than fifty years after its mailing) while going through the other letters, I found this particular envelope, held it up to the light, and saw a letter inside. It had never been opened! The letter must have arrived after Lyle was home.

Lyle arrived in St. Paul on November 29th, 1945 by train. He'd called me from San Francisco after flying there on a B-25 with a brief stop in Hawaii. Then he traveled by train from Frisco to St. Paul where we were finally in each others' arms after being apart thirty months. We spent a couple of days together before returning to Granite Falls to see his family, then to the farm near Dawson to see my family and be introduced to Lois Marie, the daughter he had never met.

The Red Cross emergency leave had saved the day. Lyle's mother lived until the following May. Lyle had three months of accumulated leave which we spent between the two family homes. He decided to accept a teaching position at the University of Minnesota College of Engineering, teaching thousands of men returning to college on the GI bill. We bought a Ford coupe and a house in Minneapolis at 932 Franklin Terrace. He began teaching the spring quarter. Lyle was honorably discharged on February 28, 1946, from Camp McCoy, Wisconsin.

On October 3, 2007, we celebrated our 65th wedding anniversary.

AN OVERVIEW of the MILITARY SERVICE of LYLE E. YOUNG IN WORLD WAR II 1943–1946

June 1942

Lyle Young was inducted into the U.S. Army as a private on June 11, 1942 at Fort Snelling, Minnesota. He applied for officer training in the Army Air Corps. His application was approved and he was sent to Chanute Field in Rantoul, Illinois, in August 1942, where he became an Aviation Cadet in a four and one-half month course culminating in his graduation on January 9, 1943, as a Second Lieutenant in the Army Air Corps. Overseas duty was expected, and after a six-month preparation and assemblage of a squadron of 230 men at military bases in Meridian, Mississippi; Venice, Florida; and Waycross, Georgia, he sailed for service in the South Pacific Theater of World War II for the following twenty-eight months.

July, 1943.

Lyle Young was an engineering officer in the 100th Service Squadron. The Squadron left Waycross, Georgia, traveling by troop train to San Francisco. On July 25, the Squadron sailed unescorted on the converted SS Taft to Townsville, Australia, on the northeastern coast of Australia. Lyle was promoted to First Lieutenant on August 9, 1943.

October, 1943.

The Squadron with housekeeping equipment moved by ship to Port Moresby, New Guinea. After a brief stay, they were transported by air over the Owen Stanley Mountains to Dobadura, near Buna, on the northeastern coast of New Guinea. (These places no longer appear on National Geographic maps.) The airplane maintenance vehicles and equipment went by ship. At Dobadura, the Squadron intensively repaired and maintained aircraft.

April, 1944.

At this point, Lt. Young was transferred to the 336th Service Squadron, which was moved by LST (Landing Ship Tank) with all its equipment to Finschhafen, (April 17-28th), and then to Aitape, New Guinea, for brief staging advances before moving by LSTs to Wakde Island, off the northern coast of New Guinea. On Wakde, the Squadron was fully operational.

September, 1944.

The 336th Service Squadron was moved by LSTs to Morotai in the Dutch East Indies (now Indonesia). The Squadron was active in its mission.

December, 1944.

The 336th moved by LSTs to Leyte, for a brief staging time before moving by LSTs to Mindora, also in the Philippines. On Mindoro, the Squadron was in full operation. Lyle was promoted to Captain on March 2, 1945.

August, 1945.

The 336th Air Service Squadron was moved to Okinawa. On August 15, 1945, Japan surrendered. The war over, the mission of the 336th Service Squadron had been completed. The slow process began of deactivating units and reassigning the men to return home.

November, 1945.

After spending almost three months in Casual Detachment units waiting for orders, Capt. Young flew back to San Francisco, and traveled by train to St. Paul, Minnesota.

February, 1946

Captain Lyle Young had three months of accumulated leave time, which he spent with his family before moving to Minneapolis, Minnesota. He was honorably discharged from the Army Air Corps on February 28, 1946, at Camp McCoy, Wisconsin.

Family Pictures

First Lieutenant Lyle Young, Army Air Corps. August 1944, in MacKay, Australia.

Captain and Mrs Lyle Young and daughter Lois Marie. November 1945.

Margie with daughter Lois Marie at six months.

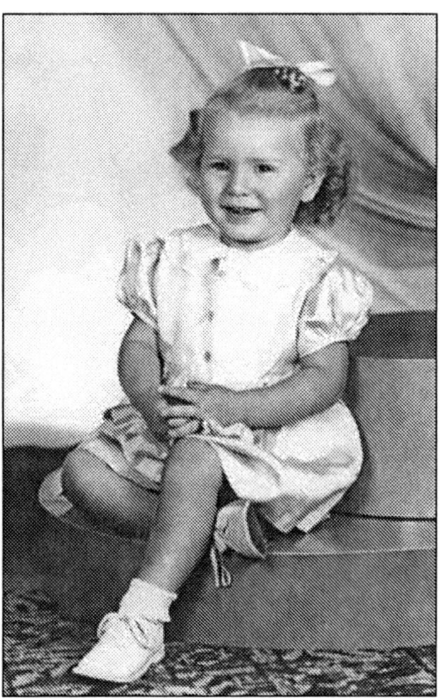

Daughter Lois Marie, November 1945. How she looked when Lyle first saw her.

EPILOGUE

Lyle Young returned home to begin a career in academia. He taught returning soldiers, known as G.I.s, in the College of Engineering at the University of Minnesota for eight years. In 1953, he moved his family to Lincoln, Nebraska, where he served as a professor and a dean in the College of Engineering and Technology until his retirement in 1986. In his retirement years he carves and paints birds, reads, plays golf, attends classes, Bible studies and church, and enjoys life with his wife Marguerite (Margie), their family and friends.

Marguerite Swenson Young is involved in volunteer activities, including church, the Osher Lifelong Learning Institute; writing classes, and keeping up with family and friends. She enjoys dressmaking and quilting. She and Lyle have loved to travel and hike in the mountains. Margie has a passion for keeping family albums and history.

Dear Reader,

Lyle and I have shared memories of an unusual time of unity in our country. Our children and our grandchildren have little knowledge of this history. We remember where we were when the Japanese bombed Pearl Harbor on December 7, 1941. We remember the years when Hitler was conquering one country after another in Europe, the bombing of London, dictators Mussolini in Italy and Stalin in Russia. We remember the battles in the Pacific from New Guinea, to the Dutch Indies, the Philippines, and to Okinawa where the heaviest naval battle of the Pacific was won.

American men were drafted and enlisted. Women enlisted in the Navy WAVES and the Army WACs, and as nurses. Unlike the first few years of the twenty-first century, the years of World War II were a time of unity. It was a war that the United States and its Allies were determined to win. Women and men worked in factories to produce the ships, the planes, the bombs, and all that was needed to supply the military. Farmers, men and women, worked to produce the foods with limited manpower as many farm men also enlisted or were drafted. Civilian goods gave way to needs of the military, and we remember the rationing of sugar, gasoline, and even shoes. No cars were manufactured for civilians.

America's young and not-so-young men became soldiers "for the duration." For service men and women overseas, there were no telephone calls back home; in the States, leaves from duty were brief; as were the "R&Rs" for rest and relaxation in faraway places. Those of us on the home front did not experience the horrors of war on the battlefields of land, air, and sea, but the loneliness, stresses of separation, and uncertainties were shared by everyone. As Lyle's letters revealed, letters were the lifeline between loved ones.

V-E Day, May 8, 1945, the day the war in Europe was over brought jubilation. But the war was still going on in the South Pacific. Americans did not know of the Manhattan Project and the secret work being done at Los Alamos, New Mexico, until after the atomic bombs were dropped on Hiroshima on August 6, and three days later at Nagasaki on August 9, 1945.

On August 15, 1945, Japan surrendered. Victory in the Pacific, V-J Day. The world rejoiced at peace across our lands. Our military men and women gradually came home to the joys of reunions and the challenges of rebuilding lives and careers. The time had come to rebuild all that war had torn asunder.

There is saying, "United we win, divided we fall." We were united, and we won.

MSY

978-0-595-47070-9
0-595-47070-X

Printed in the United States
147896LV00001BA/70/A

9 780595 470709